MISHAPS IN PARADISE

DIARY OF AN ISLAND GIRL

THE MISHAPS IN PARADISE SERIES

1. Diary of an Island Girl
2. The Pandemic

LOOK FOR MORE
MISHAPS IN PARADISE
COMING SOON!

Check our website for more details:
www.mishapsinparadise.com

Find us on:

MISHAPS
IN PARADISE

DIARY OF AN ISLAND GIRL

EVA POLIZZE

POLIZZE BOOKS

POLIZZE BOOKS

MISHAPS IN PARADISE

DIARY OF AN ISLAND GIRL

(Book 1) First Edition

Published in 2023 in Big Pine Key, Florida, U.S.A. by Polizze Books, Inc.

Library of Congress Control Number: 2022950276

HARDCOVER ISBN: 978-1-959739-00-5

PAPERBACK ISBN: 978-1-959739-01-2

E-BOOK ISBN: 978-1-959739-02-9

POLIZZE BOOKS

www.polizzebooks.com

TO OLIVIA AND CLAUDIA,
YOU ARE MY WHOLE WORLD.

SYLVIA

NATALIA

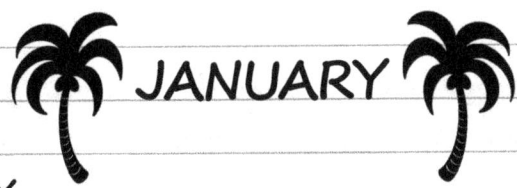

JANUARY

MONDAY

This diary belongs to a cool kid.

Okay, maybe I exaggerated with the word *cool*, but it is my diary, and I'm allowed to write whatever I want in it.

So, yes, cool is what I hope I am.

My name is Sylvia White, and I will start the dreaded middle school in the fall.

Over Christmas, we moved to the tropics where summers last all year. But we didn't move to some fascinating, big city. No, that would be too much to ask!

We moved to an island—AN ISLAND!

Imagine swaying palm trees, sandy beaches, jumping dolphins . . .

And absolutely nothing to do!!

This morning, Mom gave me this diary so I could describe my island life in "paradise."

At first, I didn't know what to write about—after all, not many exciting things happen IN MY LIFE every day.

But Mom says that life on an island is interesting and sharing feelings is good for the soul.

So, now when I write in this diary, I imagine a cool kid (like me!) reading it—someone I can totally trust with all my personal and often embarrassing confessions, someone I could be friends with for life—you!

I also decided to write this diary because, sadly, there aren't many books for girls who are not that girly.

That whole girly world isn't for me, so don't expect to see me in any dresses, ponytails, or sparkly shoes.

I wear T-shirts and shorts (or jeans) with sneakers or boots. That's it.

If you're looking to read about makeup, fashion, and girlfriends' arguments, this isn't a book for you.

Now that we have that clear, keep reading. . . .

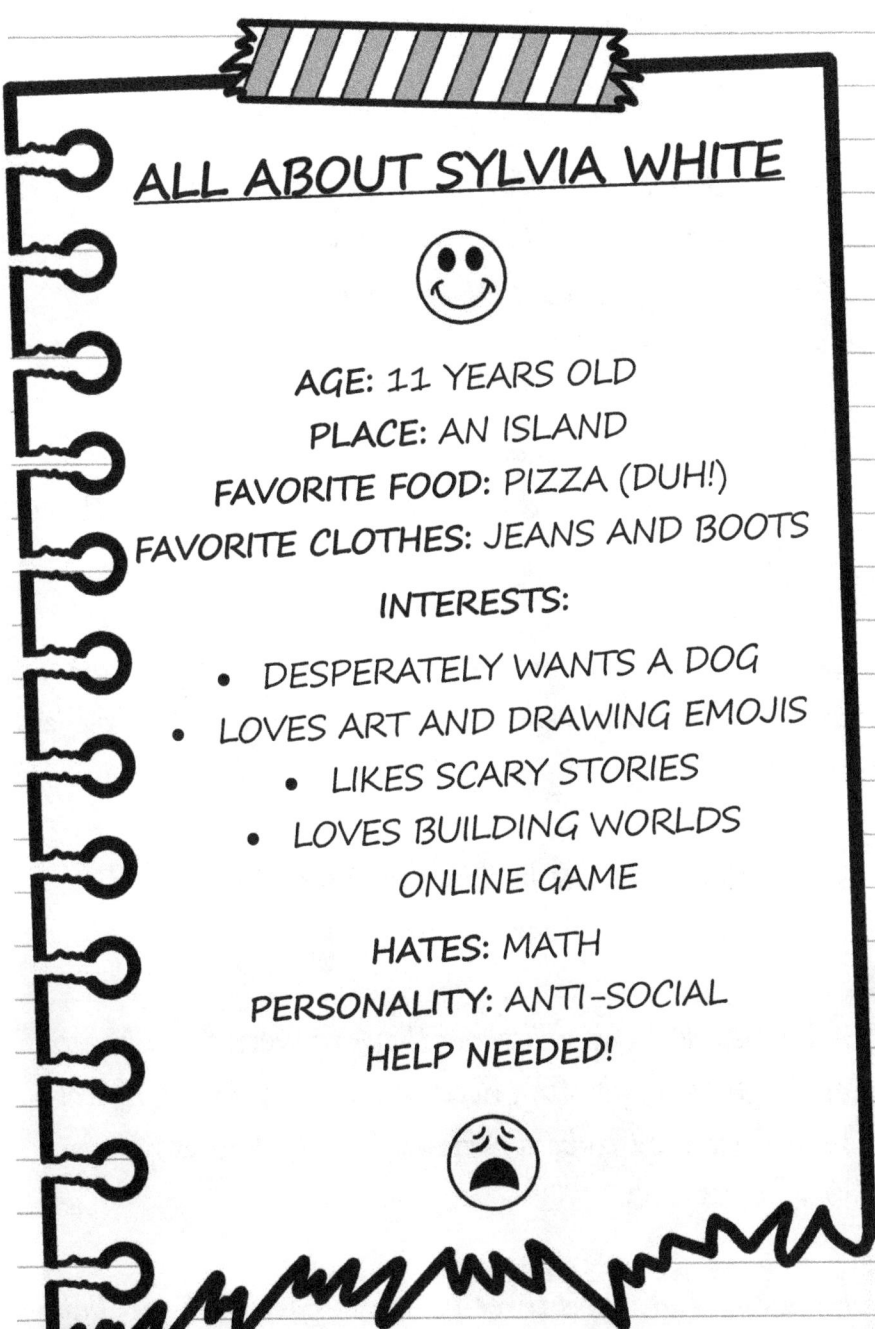

ALL ABOUT SYLVIA WHITE

AGE: 11 YEARS OLD
PLACE: AN ISLAND
FAVORITE FOOD: PIZZA (DUH!)
FAVORITE CLOTHES: JEANS AND BOOTS

INTERESTS:

- DESPERATELY WANTS A DOG
- LOVES ART AND DRAWING EMOJIS
- LIKES SCARY STORIES
- LOVES BUILDING WORLDS ONLINE GAME

HATES: MATH
PERSONALITY: ANTI-SOCIAL
HELP NEEDED!

WEDNESDAY

No diary can start without introducing you to the family, so here it comes.

Mom and Dad are pretty cool because they always put my sister and me first, no matter what. However, as Mom always points out, that doesn't mean we can do whatever we want.

Mom's life dream has always been to live in the tropics, so my parents decided to move us to the islands and give it a try.

Our NEW source of income will be three vacation houses on our island, which my parents plan to rent to travelers weekly.

They will oversee the bookings online and manage the team that will take care of everything.

A business like this will allow them to work from home, although Dad will often need to fix things in the rental homes. He used to be a carpenter, so he knows how to work with tools.

My sister, Natalia, is three years younger than me, but she genuinely believes it's the other way around.

Our DNA is the only thing we have in common, but you will learn about our differences through my diary, so there is no point in writing about it here.

You see, I have a BIG problem right now.

On Monday, Natalia and I will start going to the local island school, and I'm totally freaking out.

I'm terrified of meeting new people!

When I am around other kids, I rarely speak up for fear of saying something wrong and everyone laughing at me.

I always feel knots in my stomach whenever I am around my peers.

KNOTS IN MY STOMACH

So, meeting the island kids poses a problem for me.

A HUGE problem, I would say.

On the other hand, my sister can't wait to meet everyone because she has always been the social butterfly in our family.

Me? I'm jealous of the homeschooled kids from our church in town.

Last Sunday, I heard their stories of freedom and how their families travel to interesting places all the time.

I imagined what it would be like to be on vacation all year long—bathing in the sun under swaying palm trees, sipping fruity drinks with those cute little umbrellas—and homeschooling became my dream.

This morning, I asked Mom if I could be homeschooled, too.

She refused right away and said it wouldn't be good for my socializing since I needed to be around kids.

I tried to explain to Mom that, for me, SOCIALIZING was the NUMBER ONE reason I wanted OUT of school, but she didn't want to hear it.

Which means I'm doomed!

It looks like I'm going to the island school on Monday, after all.

FRIDAY

There are different ways you can fall.

You can fall to the ground and get hurt.

You can fall asleep and never wake up.

You can fall for a scam.

You can fall apart.

You can fall in love.

Any way you fall, the outcome is similar—you are no longer the same.

Me? I fall behind.

I'm always behind everyone around me, progressing slower than others, not getting the same results.

For this reason, I usually keep to myself to avoid everyone's questions and expectations.

As I mentioned before, I don't like drama, and I avoid it as much as possible.

When I went to my previous school, you could find me drawing something in my notebook during recess, away from everyone.

I never liked chasing games or team sports, so I kept to myself.

Kids were always picking on others, and girls argued about things I never cared about.

I used to walk in the hallways with my head down, trying to be as invisible as possible.

I rarely spoke with other kids.

But even when I said something, nobody seemed to hear me anyway, so I never felt comfortable in my own skin.

Unlike my sister, who thrives around kids.

Natalia and I have always been very different. Our differences were even more apparent when she attended kindergarten at our previous school.

Imagine two pigtails, an angelic face, a fluffy pink dress, and sparkly shoes.

Confident as always, she stood out from the crowd of terrified five-year-old kids.

From the first day of school, she became popular, and everyone her age wanted to be her friend. Go figure!

All the kindergartners wanted to sit with her during lunch.

She was always chosen first to join teams in PE, while I had to wait until most of my class was already picked.

Her friends wanted to look like her, so suddenly, little girls in pigtails surrounded us everywhere!

When Natalia went to first grade, then second grade, she continued to be very popular among kids and teachers.

But what really drove me crazy was that so many of her classmates would invite her to their birthday parties!

Do you know what that meant for me?

Mom always took me with her, so I spent every weekend with thirty little kids who were three years younger than me!

Don't get me wrong—sometimes it was fun when families rented those giant waterslides.

But they always made me watch the little ones so they wouldn't hurt themselves, while all I wanted to do was zoom right past them!

However, I always made the day worth it by grabbing a large piece of cake and explaining that older kids needed bigger desserts to fill their larger bellies.

I don't know if they really believed my theory because they always looked at me suspiciously.

Unlike me, Natalia is an excellent student, so she always becomes all the teachers' favorite.

She is one of those students who goes the extra mile to please her teachers, collecting all the little award star stickers and earning rewards left and right. (I'm rolling my eyes here.)

Natalia never seemed to fear anything, even when she was a little kid.

I remember when Mom wanted to introduce her to math when Natalia was just four years old.

Mom printed out a single sheet of paper with basic, simple math addition equations from zero to ten.

She put it in front of Natalia and said, "You don't have to be scared."

My little sister looked at her, confused. "Why would I be scared of a paper?"

I'm not as confident as my sister.

What I really dread about school is being around all the bullies.

Don't get me wrong—some girls were nice to me in my previous school.

But most of the kids always looked for reasons to roll their eyes at me, shake their heads every time I tried to answer a teacher's question, or simply comment on everything I did with sarcasm in their voices.

Their behavior completely shut me down, so I don't think I can ever speak in public again.

Or be comfortable making friends . . .

"You've got to open up, Sylvia," Mom said this morning.

"Don't count on it," I murmured.

I don't know why I need to be social.

What if I feel happy the way I am?

Why can't a loner be left . . . well, . . . alone?

SUNDAY

Because I've always had freezing cold winters all my life, it's crazy for me to experience summer in January.

While snow covers half of the world, I am on a raft, floating in OUR own pool!

HOW COOL IS THAT?

Our new waterfront, five-bedroom house sits on a one-acre lot with a pool and a tiki hut in the backyard. We also have a swing set, a trampoline, and a treehouse. Our new boat is docked at the dock, and we even have a private pier!

Tropical trees and palms grow along the perimeter of the entire property, so we have privacy all around.

Mom's dream has always been to have a big house, a large lot, and complete privacy from the neighbors.

Like me, Mom likes to be secluded from people, so it's surprising that she pushes me to make friends with other kids.

I'm perfectly fine with just online friends who join me to play my favorite game on the internet—BUILDING WORLDS.

Anyway, I don't tell you this to brag about our property—I tell you this so you know my parents bought a great place for kids, making living in the tropics more exciting.

Unfortunately, not everything looks so idyllic in paradise.

Although our island has a small mall with:

- a food store,
- a clothing store,
- a post office,
- a few restaurants,
- and a church nearby,

this place is so far away from NORMAL civilization that I'm worried about surviving here.

But, apparently, that's what tourists LOVE about vacationing in the islands—being away from the noises and crowds of big cities.

Massive bridges connect the main islands nearby, so we don't have to take a boat everywhere. Thank goodness!

Can you imagine?

Although we can use a car to leave the islands and go to the mainland, we are hours away from any major city.

Which means I'm doomed.

To be honest, I would switch places with anyone who lives in a busy metropolitan area with cool subways, tramcars, and millions of options to go shopping, eat, and have fun.

But Mom says we are fortunate to live in paradise, and many people in the world would switch places with me in a heartbeat.

As an eleven-year-old kid, I can't see how living away from movie theaters, amusement parks, and giant malls can be fun, but I guess you need to be a grown-up to appreciate being cut off from everything.

So, because I can't easily pack up and leave this place, wish me good luck. I will need it for sure!

Especially tomorrow—on the first day at the island school.

MONDAY

Today was our first day at the island school, and I could describe it with just one word: SHOCKING!

The school is within walking distance of our house, but Mom wanted to give us a ride on the first day.

During our quick car ride, we saw an alligator crossing the street right in front of us!

AN ALLIGATOR CROSSING THE STREET!!

Mom had to hit the brakes not to run him over!

I don't know what animals freely roam where you live, but **I AM DEFINITELY NOT OKAY** with alligators strolling near my house!!

"Well, that was unexpected," Mom said when the reptile disappeared into the bushes.

"You think?" I asked, still in shock. "Maybe we should have researched the islands BEFORE we moved here?"

"I'm sure we will be fine . . . But I will be taking you to school in my car. Just in case . . ." Mom said and smiled.

I didn't find it funny.

As soon as Mom pulled into the school parking lot, I couldn't believe how small the building was!

The school has both elementary and middle school in one building, which means Natalia and I will spend years in this place!

Besides the size of the building, I liked that the school's outside walls were decorated with kids' art.

"Sylvia, look at the amazing paintings," Mom said. "I'm sure you will add yours, too."

I nodded. "That would be cool."

I love art because I find it easier to communicate with drawings than with words.

"Did I tell you they have a special art department at this school?" Mom said. "They even have a pottery studio!"

"Really?" I looked at the school and smiled. Maybe attending it won't be as bad as I thought.

"I can't wait to meet everyone!" Natalia said with excitement in her voice.

Mom kissed us on our cheeks. "Have fun, enjoy, and always think positive."

When we entered the school, we found ourselves in a cafeteria where many kids were screaming and goofing around.

I was grateful for this chaos because nobody seemed to notice the two new students standing in the hallway.

And being invisible when you are new at school is a good thing, trust me!

But as soon as I looked around, I knew I didn't fit in. Everyone wore summer clothes, while I wore jeans and boots!

I directed Natalia to her table with a sign for second grade, then I sat down at the fifth-grade table and prayed nobody would pay me any mind.

And nobody did.

Soon, teachers from each grade came and lined up their students to walk them to their classrooms.

Mrs. Clark, my new fifth-grade teacher, had a friendly smile when she approached me. "You must be Sylvia."

I nodded.

"Welcome to our island school. I know you will like it here very much."

I wasn't sure about that, but I said nothing.

When we entered the classroom, Mrs. Clark asked me to stand next to her desk to introduce myself in front of the ENTIRE class.

Great! Forget about my plan to sneak into the farthest desk from the teacher, unnoticed!

I don't know why teachers do that to new students.

Many people consider public speaking to be the most stressful thing; yet, at school, they make you speak in front of everyone like it's a piece of cake.

"Um . . . My name is Sylvia White . . ." Okay, what else should I say? "I come from the freezing North."

"Can you tell us something interesting about yourself?" Mrs. Clark asked, putting me on the spot AGAIN.

I shrugged. "Nothing is interesting about me."

I thought my answer would end my introduction, but I was wrong. Several kids raised their hands and started asking questions.

"Will you miss wearing hats, scarves, and gloves?"

"Um . . . no," I said. Does anyone ever miss being cold?

"What does snow feel like?"

Nobody had ever asked me that question, but then again, I had never met anyone who hadn't seen snow before, either.

"It's fluffy," I said.

"Have you ever ice skated?"

I did. In fourth grade, I received ice skates for Christmas, so the next day, I went to an ice-skating rink and tried my best not to get killed by everyone bumping into me while my legs went in opposite directions.

No matter how much I practiced turning, I couldn't control where I was going, and I ended up crashing into the side of the rink. After that, I had bruises all over my body and needed medical attention.

"Yes, I ice skated, and I did all right," I said. Who really needs to know the details, right?

"Thank you, Sylvia," Mrs. Clark said. "Please take your seat at the desk I've prepared for you."

I nodded and walked toward the empty desk at the end of the classroom.

At least I was far from the teacher, just like I preferred.

Out of sight, out of mind.

When I sat down, a girl next to me leaned toward me and whispered, "If you still have your winter hat, gloves, and scarf, and you aren't gonna use them, can I have them?"

The girl had a completely different fashion style than me.

She was wearing a fancy blouse, colorful leggings, and sandals. She'd decorated herself with handmade bracelets and a beaded necklace.

With her dark brown, curly hair, plus artsy earrings in her ears, she looked like a true fashionista.

Unlike me. My hair is blond, long, and straight, and I do absolutely nothing to style it.

In my jeans, a comfortable T-shirt, and boots, I may look like I'm ready to conquer the world, but in reality, I just want to crawl into a shell and hide.

"Why would you need my stuff?" I asked when the teacher wasn't looking.

"I've never had those."

"You've never been cold before?" I asked, surprised.

"Nope."

I smiled. "Okay. I'll bring them tomorrow."

"GIRLS!" Mrs. Clark said, looking straight at us. "Leave the chitchat for after class, please."

The girl next to me giggled. "Sorry, ma'am."

After the lesson was over (if I had only paid attention to what it was about!), the girl next to me came to my desk and extended her hand. "I'm Tracy."

I shook it. "Sylvia." But she already knew that.

Before she could say anything else, another girl approached my desk. "Are you going to war with those boots?" she asked with a smirk on her face.

I could hear other girls laughing.

"Mind your own business!" Tracy said, then turned toward me when the other girls walked away. "Don't pay any mind to her and her SQUAD. That's Brittany, and everyone considers her to be the most beautiful girl in our class, which she is very aware of."

I could see why . . . She had long dark hair that curled up at the bottom.

Because she wore sandals like most of the girls around here, I noticed she had a manicure and a pedicure done, while I had never even been to a salon.

She wore fashionable brand-name clothes from stores I had never even heard of before.

Now, don't get me wrong—I'm not complaining. I have never been very girly or interested in stuff like that.

But when you stand next to a model-looking girl like Brittany, you tend to rethink your own clothing choices.

Maybe I dress too boyishly? I only wear T-shirts and jeans, or shorts. Should I be wearing blouses and skirts? Will I ever fit in at this island school where everyone seems to enjoy flowery summer clothes?

Tracy sighed. "Brittany can be such a pain sometimes. It's best to ignore her."

I nodded. "Got it."

Later, Tracy showed me around the school, which was even smaller than I had thought, and the rest of the day passed uneventfully.

When we walked by the second-grade classroom, I noticed Natalia talking and laughing with a bunch of girls, all mesmerized by my little sister.

It doesn't matter where she goes—she always steals everyone's hearts.

I imagined what it would be like not to have the knots in my stomach when I was around other kids.

What it would be like to breathe freely instead of holding everything inside me.

What it would be like to speak up every time someone criticized me.

What it would be like not to be afraid . . .

😔

TUESDAY

The subject I dreaded the most was PE class, which was today!

This morning, I asked Mom if she could write a note to the PE teacher saying that I had some kind of unexplainable disease and I should be excused from doing any sports.

But, as always, Mom didn't want to hear it.

She says it's important for us to do sports and be active.

Natalia, of course, was very excited and couldn't wait for her first PE class!

Sometimes, I don't know about this child!

"What does PE stand for?" Natalia asked me in the car on the way to school.

"Pointless Exercise," I said.

"Sylvia, stop!" Mom reacted. "You will like it, I promise."

Well, I didn't like it!

My first PE class was a nightmare!

At this island school, all same-grade classrooms have PE together, boys and girls, which means I had to deal with another fifth-grade class full of unfamiliar kids.

Then, the coach, Mr. Baloony, announced there would be schoolwide RELAY RACES WITH A BATON at the end of February, and for the following weeks, he would be training us to work in teams.

"Every student at school must participate," he said. "Each grade will have eight teams with four runners, and the fastest three teams from each grade will get medals. I will watch how you all perform during PE classes, and the eight students who excel in sports will choose their teams. You can end up with ANYONE, so you all had better work on your teamwork skills."

I hate running! I hate sweating! I hate races, competitions, and championships!

GET ME OUT OF THIS SCHOOL!!

This is just my luck!

It's bad enough that I have to go to a new school with kids I don't know. Now I have to compete in sports and team up with total strangers!

The first teamwork training started today, and I even struggled to understand the rules of the game!

We were all positioned in different spots on the field outside of the school, and someone threw a small ball, but I wasn't sure what to do with it!

I mean, I was pretty sure we were not playing soccer—I would recognize that type of ball.

There were no hoops, so this couldn't be a basketball game.

No net across the field, so it wasn't volleyball.

So, what game were we playing??

I was so stressed out I could hardly breathe!

Tracy stood on the opposite side of the field, so I couldn't ask her what kind of game this was.

I must have looked lost because I saw Brittany laughing at me and shaking her head.

I was hoping I could watch the kids play a little, and maybe I would figure it out, but NO, one boy from the other fifth-grade class had to make me feel welcome, and he threw the ball at me right away!!

As the ball was approaching, I had a few options: either take it, kick it, run with it (but where?), or simply ignore it.

I chose the last one. As soon as the ball neared me, I scooted away to let it pass me.

And believe it or not, they screamed for joy!

"YAY!!"

I don't know what they were playing, but apparently, we scored, and I became the new hero of the day.

Everyone congratulated me, and I was like, "Sure, no problem. Anytime."

For the rest of the game, I kept running away from the ball, which seemed to do the trick because our team won!

After the game, the boy who threw the ball at me first approached me and said, "That wasn't so bad, was it?"

He had brown, unruly hair and a pleasant smile.

I shook my head. "No, it wasn't."

He extended his hand to me. "I'm Alex."

I shook his hand. "Sylvia," I said in a faint voice because these things are never easy for me.

He smiled. "I've never seen you around. Are you new?"

"Yes. It's my second day. . . ."

"Cool. I take it you're from up North because your skin is so white."

I laughed. "Yes."

Alex looked at me with curiosity in his eyes, which made me uncomfortable. "Welcome to our school. If you ever get lost in the hallways, I'll be happy to help you."

I burst out laughing. "You're kidding me, right? You can't get lost in such a small school. There is like . . . literally nowhere to go."

My previous school had several buildings, and we needed a map to find our classrooms during the first week of school.

Alex smiled. "Well, you know where to find me . . . just in case."

"Thanks."

After that, more kids came over to me and introduced themselves.

I couldn't remember all their names, but it was the first time so many human beings had any interest in getting to know me.

If dodging a ball does the trick, then I may start liking PE classes, after all.

Okay, fine, I will admit—some kids were nice.

But nothing will change the fact that

I REALLY HATE SPORTS!!

While sitting together during lunch, I handed Tracy my winter hat, scarf, and gloves.

I had never worn those items because they had colorful stripes on them. I kept my black set at home in case we would ever travel up North again.

"COOL!" Tracy said. "I love the colors! Thank you!"

"No problem," I said and started eating a warm slice of pizza from the cafeteria.

When she finished her lunch, Tracy put the gloves on her hands and the hat on her head, then wrapped the scarf around her neck.

And she kept wearing them for the rest of the day.

Inside the school.
On a hot day.
In the tropics.

Maybe I will fit in at this island school, after all.

WEDNESDAY

When Tracy came to school today, she surprised me by wearing my winter hat, gloves, and scarf again.

But no one, besides me, considered it to be strange. It seems as if everyone is used to Tracy fashioning all kinds of outfits at school.

"Have you seriously never worn winter clothes before?" I asked her during lunch.

She shook her head. "Born and raised in the islands by parents who have no desire to go anywhere else."

"Does it bother you?"

"No. I like where I live . . . but it would be nice to wear those tall boots from time to time."

I smiled. "You know, those warm outfits come at a price—it's usually freezing cold outside when you wear them."

"I can't even imagine what it feels like," she said and took a bite of her sandwich.

"It feels as if your toes and fingers are about to fall off from numbness while you are trying to breathe with icicles in your nose."

Tracy nodded. "COOL!"

I smiled. I had a feeling Tracy was my kind of girl.

"I can give you my tall boots, too, because I never wear those. I only like these combat boots," I said, pointing to my shoes.

"Really? Awesome! I will wear them for the Winter Dance at our school," she said.

"Winter Dance? What's that?"

"Every year at the end of January, our school has a party in the cafeteria, called the Winter Dance, to celebrate the coldest month in the islands. We islanders enjoy the breeze that January brings," Tracy said and smiled.

I burst out laughing. "You all celebrate the winter, which you DON'T have."

"What are you talking about? It is winter, no matter what. And it's not as hot as it is in the summer. And the ocean is colder."

"So, everyone celebrates the break from the heat. Is that what you're saying?"

"Exactly! You'll have fun."

"I'm not planning to go to any dances. I don't wear dresses and fancy shoes. And I certainly don't dance."

"Sylvia, you can't stay home!"

"Trust me. I can," I said and got up because the lunch break was over.

Just in time, thank goodness.

I cannot imagine myself in a dress, let alone DANCING!

SATURDAY

Let me tell you, being around your MOM isn't always all that fun.

Moms tend to embarrass us kids every step of the way.

They teach us how to behave and what to say in different situations, but, if you ask me, sometimes they have no clue themselves!

Today, the school organized a geography fair for our families. The theme of the fair was "Islands Around the World."

Students who wanted to attend the fair needed to prepare presentation boards about an island of their choice and come to school with their parents and siblings in the evening.

So, of course, Mom made us sign up to attend the event, no matter how much I begged her to let me stay home.

In the end, Natalia and I decided to make a presentation board about Hawaii.

At first, we didn't want to do it, so we asked Mom if she could do the job for us, but she refused, which wasn't a surprise.

She said since we're online a lot anyway, we might as well use that time to do something useful and research Hawaii for the project.

As you can see, Mom really knows how to remove the fun from things sometimes.

I'm not big on researching things on the internet unless we're talking about cute puppies, poodle moths, or scary stories, so this task definitely caught me off-guard.

I decided to focus on the basics: the map to show where Hawaii is located on the globe and the food the islands are famous for.

That's all anyone really needs to know, and Natalia agreed since I was in charge.

The first surprising fact I learned while researching was that Hawaii, although a part of the United States of America, is not geographically located in North America!

The islands of Hawaii are a part of Polynesia and are grouped together with the continent of Australia under one name: Oceania.

So, we glued a world map on the board and pointed to Hawaii's location in the Pacific Ocean.

Then we added pictures of *poi*, a thick paste made from taro root, and *laulau*, pork and fish wrapped in taro leaves.

After that, I needed to research what taro was, and it turned out to be an edible plant with large leaves grown in Hawaii and other Polynesian islands.

Next, we glued photos of the *kalua pig* dish and *poke*, which is a raw fish cut into bite-sized cubes.

And of course, we couldn't forget about the pineapple!

I figured if people knew that much, they would do just fine!

But, of course, Mom said it wasn't enough.

She told me to research the flag, the capital, the population, the landmarks, and a bit of history.

Boring!

I disagreed with Mom because, in my opinion, tourists traveling to Hawaii need to know where it is and what they can eat there.

But, as always, Mom made me do extra things.

First of all, it's hard to research information about Hawaii because the names in the Hawaiian language are extremely difficult to read or pronounce.

For example, the Hawaii state fish is the **Humuhumunukunukuāpua'a.**

Go ahead. Read the word. I will wait here.

The funny thing is that the fish is tiny, and it's not even edible! You would think, if they name an animal with such a long word, at least it should be the size of a blue whale, which is the largest animal in the world!

But then again, I shouldn't be surprised by their difficult words because I learned that the Hawaiian language has only thirteen letters!

No wonder most words in Hawaiian are tongue twisters and sound similar.

At the end of the day, I memorized only two Hawaiian words: *Aloha*, which means hello, goodbye, or love, and *Mahalo*, which means thank you.

After two ADDITIONAL hours of gluing down more information about Hawaii, the presentation board was finally done, and we were ready for the fair.

But, as soon as we arrived at school, things didn't go as planned.

I hoped to set up my station near Tracy, who had made a board about the Bahamas. But she must have gotten there much earlier because all the spots near her were taken by the time we got there.

So now I was stuck near people I'd never seen before, like seventh and eighth graders.

Tracy has been wearing my winter hat, gloves, and scarf to school every day, and today wasn't any different.

I waved to her, letting her know I was there, and she waved back, although her attention quickly went to the kids standing in front of her table.

You see, we were supposed to display our boards on the table and represent our station for some time, answering questions about the island to anyone who visited us.

Kids collected stickers from each island on their "passports" for a chance to win a "world traveler" backpack.

But, shortly after Natalia and I got everything set up and ready to go, I had a strong urge to go to the restroom.

I think it was my nerves that got me going. Being around so many strangers gives me anxiety, and I always need to go to the bathroom when it happens.

Unfortunately, someone was inside the girls' restroom, and when I knocked, the woman said she would be there for a while.

So, I knew I had to tough this one out.

I paced back and forth for a little bit, trying to see if I could "squeeze" things back inside so I could return to the fair.

Unfortunately, there was no way I was holding anything in at this point, as my mind was already set on going full force.

I figured the only way was to go to the boys' restroom.

GROSS!

I dreaded going there, but nature's call was way too strong.

I quietly entered the boys' restroom and looked around to check if anyone was there. Phew! It was empty.

As soon as I locked the door, someone knocked, and I said, "Occupied!" But then, I covered my mouth with my hand because I realized a girl's voice had come out from a boys' restroom! GREAT!

When I got myself all comfortable, a message spoken over the speakers throughout the entire school startled me:

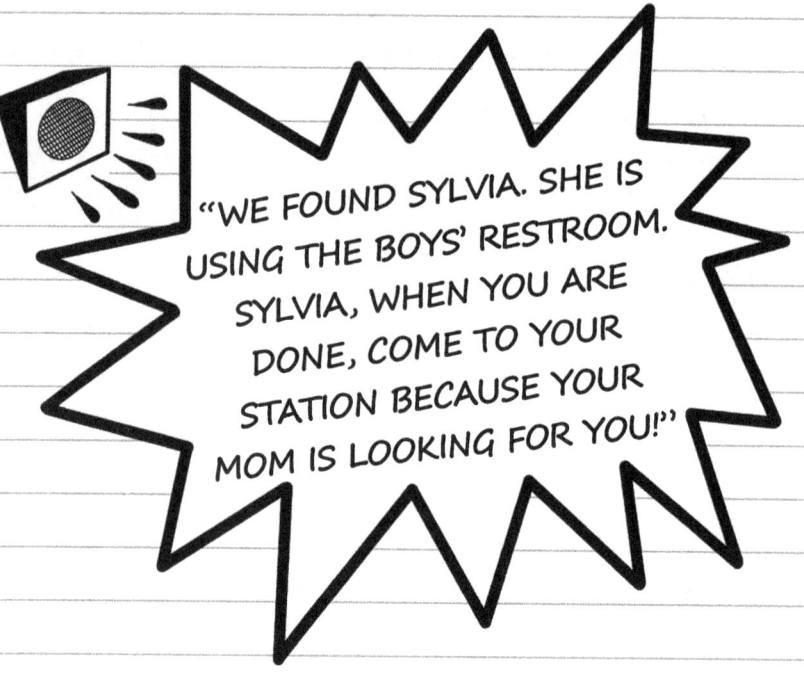

"WE FOUND SYLVIA. SHE IS USING THE BOYS' RESTROOM. SYLVIA, WHEN YOU ARE DONE, COME TO YOUR STATION BECAUSE YOUR MOM IS LOOKING FOR YOU!"

These are the moments when bringing your parents to school is a mistake because one of them is always there with you, embarrassing you in front of everyone.

I seriously considered staying in that restroom for eternity so I could be spared the jokes and laughter that would surely follow a message like that. But everyone already knew where I was, so it was pointless.

When I sneaked back to our station, most of the geography fair was done, and everyone was congregating in the middle of the room, talking and laughing.

Since I saw Brittany in the center of the kids, looking at me with a smirk on her face, I was sure they had laughed at me, so I decided not to "visit" other kids' display boards. Which meant I didn't get a reward for being a "world traveler"—a cool backpack!

But guess who did! Natalia, of course!

And this is the reason I WILL NOT be attending the geography fair next year for sure!

And I'm not looking forward to going back to school on Monday!

I just don't fit in!

The only nice thing that happened today was when someone left a plate on my table with all kinds of desserts from different islands.

A note next to the plate read:

> Sylvia,
> Sorry you don't feel good, and you missed the fair.
> I gathered the sweets from every island at the fair for you.
> Hope it will make you feel better.
>
> A.

I asked my sister if she knew who had left the pastries for me, but she said she was away from the table, visiting the other displays (of course she was!) and didn't see who had brought it.

In my mind, I ran through all the names in my class, trying to figure out who it was.

I knew it wasn't Tracy because her name started with a "T."

There was Alice. But we had never spoken before, so why would she do such a thing?

If it wasn't Alice, then the only person whose name started with an "A" was . . . Alex.

Could the boy who threw the ball to me in PE be the one who left the desserts on my table?

SUNDAY

Today, I invited Tracy to come to our place.

While we were lounging by the pool on this beautiful Sunday morning, all Tracy talked about was middle school.

"I wonder what it will be like to be a middle schooler," she said.

I sighed. "I don't feel mature enough to be in middle school yet," I said.

And it's true. I still feel like a kid, and I don't think I'm ready for this next step.

Don't middle schoolers need to behave more maturely? Think more responsibly? Know how to behave and what to say in every situation?

Well, I definitely don't.

"Do you feel ready?" I asked her.

"Yes! I can't wait!" she said.

"Really? Why?"

"I will meet new people from other islands who will join our school and have my own locker! How cool is that? I'm already planning how I will decorate it."

"Aren't you even a little nervous about meeting all those unfamiliar faces?"

She shook her head. "No, I'm excited about it. Weren't you when you met everyone at our island school?"

"No! I was terrified!" I said.

"Not even a little bit?"

"Okay, maybe there was this one exciting moment when someone left pastries on my table during the geography fair. . . ."

Tracy raised herself to a sitting position and looked at me directly. "Who was it?"

"There was only an initial 'A' on the note. I think it was one of the boys. . . ."

The corners of Tracy's mouth lifted in a bright smile. "A BOY? And you didn't tell me right away?"

I felt my cheeks blush. "I'm not really 100% sure it was him. . . ."

"Him?" she asked, digging for more information.

"Alex from the other fifth-grade class. He was kind of nice to me during the first PE class."

Tracy plopped herself back onto the lounge chair. "Sylvia, never keep details like these away from me! This is so cool!"

"What's cool?"

"I know Alex, and I can tell you one thing—I wish all the boys in our class were nice like him. I hope they will mature by the time middle school starts. I really would like to have a male friend one day. My older cousin says that friendship with a boy can be helpful to understand boys in general."

"Really?" I never thought about it. To be honest, I haven't thought about boys much so far. To me, they have always been some kind of different species or something.

"Absolutely! This way, when you fall in love one day, you will have a male friend to guide you, you know?"

"What if you fall in love with the *boy* friend?"

Tracy burst out laughing. "I don't know. If you fall in love with your friend, you can't ask him for advice on love matters. But anyway, Alex may be as shy as you are if he only put his initial on the note. You should get to know him better. . . ."

I smiled, but in reality, I felt even more nervous inside.

A boy? Me? Friendship?

I'm not ready for this!

A few minutes later, when we sat at the edge of the pool, sipping lemonades, she asked me the question I had been dreading.

"Do you think we should have some kind of middle school goal before middle school starts in the fall?" she said.

"What do you mean by MIDDLE SCHOOL GOAL?" I asked.

"You know, some kind of big change, something different about us, a new plan, or . . . maybe a new look?"

"What's wrong with what I look like now?" I asked, puzzled.

"Nothing. But it would be nice to have . . . a new goal. Something middle school worthy."

There it was. The CHANGE I was worried about. The CHANGE that meant showing you are growing up, something new to differentiate us from the elementary kids.

"Do I have to have a plan? Do I have to change? I kind of like the way I am. . . ." I said.

I really don't like changes. I don't have a plan for middle school. And, apart from wanting a dog, I don't really have any major goals right now. Is something wrong with me?

Tracy smiled. "I think we both should. What could we do?"

"Hmm . . . I don't know . . ."

"How about we'll think about our MIDDLE SCHOOL GOAL, and we'll discuss what we have chosen this week?" she asked.

"Okay," I said, but inside I was screaming:

I DON'T LIKE CHANGE!

I'm still so childish, which I like, by the way.

Should I be more serious?

Should I change something about myself to get ready for middle school?

For a friendship with a BOY?

Every time I do something silly, Mom and Dad tell me I'm too old to behave like that, or it's not a middle school thing.

Does it have to be?

My uncles and aunts have recently been asking me what my plan is for middle school, too.

Do I have to have one?

How about not growing up?

MONDAY

All morning, I've been thinking about that MIDDLE SCHOOL GOAL Tracy and I discussed yesterday.

Maybe I *should* have a new goal for middle school. . . . A new plan . . .

I don't know about you, but I imagine myself filthy rich in the future.

Not like my parents are, but more!

My parents say they are not rich at all, just "fortunate."

Mom says rich people have plenty of money to spend on their everyday needs. They can afford maids, chauffeurs, and chefs. They spoil themselves with fancy cars and luxurious vacations.

My parents are "invested," which means they worked hard when they were younger, stripped themselves of all the luxuries, and invested their money in homes they rent to people.

So, although they receive money from people every week, they need to give it back to the bank that had given them loans to buy the houses at the beginning.

This makes little sense to me because I don't know how they make money this way.

Mom says that although we are fortunate to have a nice property, we don't have liquid cash to spend on luxuries, which means we are not rich at all. Just invested and fortunate (that word again!).

First of all, I don't understand how cash can be liquid. From my experience, I know it can't!

Mom often forgets to remove dollars from Dad's pockets before doing his laundry. And since I am aware of this, I always volunteer to fold his clothes so I can be the first one to find the cash and keep it!

"Finders, keepers; losers, weepers," I say when I tell them about the money.

It's usually only a few dollars, so they let me have it, especially since I fold the clothes.

But, no matter how long the bills are in the washing machine soaking in water, they never turn to liquid!

Fortunately for me, the bills are perfectly fine!

When I grow up, I would like to have people helping me around the house because I feel sad when I watch my parents working hard on our property.

Dad cares for the lawn himself, trims all the palm trees, and cleans the pool. Mom does all the landscaping herself and cleans the house.

Of course, my sister and I help Mom with the house, but to be honest, we always dread it.

I wish we could afford help because it's great to have a large house, but cleaning it is not fun at all! In that case, you kind of wish you just had a small apartment and called it a day.

So, my plan is to save as much money as possible during my childhood so that by the time I'm a grown-up, I will have a great start on the way to wealth, and I can afford to hire people to do domestic stuff for me.

Since I don't play with toys anymore, and I don't care about fashion, my relatives usually give me money for birthdays and special occasions.

But with only a few holidays here and there, it's hard to get anywhere, if you know what I mean.

So, I decided my plan for middle school should be . . . to earn money on my own!

Yes! That will be my MIDDLE SCHOOL GOAL!

I told Tracy about my plan during lunch at school.

"I like it! That's a responsible middle school thing. This way, you can ask Alex out for ice cream," she said and smiled.

Leave it to Tracy to have boys on her mind. "I was kind of planning to spend it on maids, chauffeurs, and private chefs."

She laughed. "I came up with my MIDDLE SCHOOL GOAL, too!"

"Okay, what is it?"

Tracy adjusted the scarf I'd given to her around her neck. She still wore my winter hat and gloves, but everyone was used to it by now. "Definitely a new look!

I don't want to look the same in my school photos in middle school. I have to look different! I mean . . . it's just common sense!"

Ugh. Fashion! Great! The only fashion choice I make every day is what T-shirt and shorts I should wear.

Tracy continued, "I'm thinking about straightening my hair more often. I would look completely different."

"What's wrong with your curls? You have, like, the most beautiful curly hair ever!"

"Ugh, thanks . . . But I still would like to look different . . . all grown up!"

"I have completely straight hair. I don't feel grown up at all," I said.

Tracy burst out laughing. "Maybe you should curl your hair then."

"No, thanks. I'm staying with the GETTING RICH plan," I said.

"You're silly," Tracy said and laughed.

SILLY is my thing for sure!

TUESDAY

Just as I was already thinking that maybe going to the island school would be fun, THIS HAPPENED!

During PE, Coach said that both fifth-grade classes would play volleyball to practice working as a team.

At first, I was happy that I knew what we would play this time.

He divided us into two groups, and I was glad to see Tracy by my side.

The boy named Alex was on the opposite team, and he stood behind the net—right in front of me, looking straight into my eyes!

I felt my cheeks burning, and I remembered the desserts on my table during the geography fair.

I wanted to ask him if he was the one who had left them there, but so many kids were around us. . . . I was too shy to ask.

What if it wasn't him? I would completely embarrass myself if I assumed wrong.

Every time Alex looked in my direction, my legs turned to cotton, and I couldn't focus on the game.

So, knowing what we were playing didn't help me at all because I was as clumsy as if I had no clue anyway.

What's worse, Brittany was also on the opposite team, and she made it her mission to throw the ball AT ME every chance she could.

She knew very well that I was TERRIBLE at sports and that her team would win if the ball passed me every time.

Which it did, and we were losing miserably.

And just when I thought things couldn't get any worse, Brittany spiked the ball toward me with such a speed that it hit my head, and I collapsed to the ground.

I don't know how long I was lying there unconscious, but when I opened my eyes, everyone was gathered around me.

Well, besides Brittany, of course, who showed no remorse at all.

It surprised me to see Alex squatting beside me with a worried face. "Are you okay?" he asked.

I nodded, although I wasn't sure.

Then I saw Brittany frown and walk away.

Coach called the nurse, who called my mom, and within an hour, I was home, lying in my bed, sipping on a hot chocolate.

"I told you I'm physically challenged," I said to Mom when she hovered around me, caring for my every want and need.

"Don't be ridiculous. You are a healthy, beautiful young girl. It's all in your mind," she answered.

"I'm lucky I'm not braindead after this PE class!"

"You will be fine," she said and walked out of my room.

But what if something happened to my brain after the ball hit my head? At least now, there would be a reason I'm different from everyone else.

Maybe I can use this as an excuse not to attend PE anymore.

CLINICALLY DISTURBED, Mom would explain. OVERREACTIVE FEAR OF BALLS.

Hey, it's worth a shot!

WEDNESDAY

No matter how much I begged Mom to let me stay home for a few days to RECUPERATE from my BRAIN INJURY, she told me to go to school and get back on the horse.

When I mentioned I might have a POSTDRAMATIC STRESS DISORDER, she didn't want to hear any of my excuses.

She said I should be happy I was a healthy child and that some people had real health issues and couldn't do all those things I could.

I dreaded returning to school because I felt like I disappointed all my classmates during the game, and Brittany embarrassed me in front of Alex and everyone else during PE.

"I'm so happy you're okay," Tracy said during lunch. "I was so worried."

"Thanks, I'm okay, although I would prefer to be injured so I don't have to go to PE classes ever again."

"You don't mean that. Besides, Alex has PE with us."

"Yeah. He probably thinks I'm a total dork!"

"He does not. He looked worried about you when you left with your mom."

"He did?"

Tracy nodded. "Yes. I think he would like to get to know you more. You should join our Art Club. We have workshops after school once a week, and we do all kinds of cool things there. And . . . Alex comes, too."

"Really? He likes art?" I asked. I enjoyed the art classes during school hours, but I wasn't aware there was an Art Club I could join and do more creative stuff.

"Yes. He comes every week. Unfortunately . . . so does Brittany."

Of course! Life just can't get easy for me!

As if on cue, Brittany came over to our table and smiled. "I'm sorry I hit you in the head yesterday. But think on the bright side—at least now you don't have to explain to anyone why you are so weird."

I opened my mouth to say something, but before I lowered myself to Brittany's level, I heard someone else's voice.

"Leave her alone," Alex said with a stern look on his face.

Brittany shrugged and left.

"Are you okay?" he asked me.

When nothing was coming out of my mouth, Tracy nudged me.

"Yes . . . thank you," I said.

Alex nodded and walked away.

What I REALLY don't like about this school is that I'm going through such a rollercoaster every day.

On the one hand, I dread coming here in the mornings; on the other hand, I hate to leave in the afternoons.

I would be ecstatic if I never saw Brittany again, but I would miss hanging out with Tracy and . . . seeing Alex.

THURSDAY

Today was a record-breaking low temperature in the islands—45°F, about 7°C. I don't know where you live in the world, but this temperature feels like a cold fall day.

And yet, everyone at school panicked.

Kids came bundled up in thin sweatshirts and rain jackets. Nobody seemed to have any REAL winter clothes, and the building had no heating system, so everyone trembled all day.

Nobody was happy to go outside for recess today, so most of the kids walked in circles around the playground, trying to stay warm.

It was funny to see kids stressing over a chilly day; but then again, I wore jeans, boots, a heavy sweater, and my winter jacket, which kept me warm and comfortable.

And it seemed like everyone was jealous of me today.

But it surprised me that Tracy hated the cold weather.

We were sitting under a palm tree when I told her, "Of all people, you should be happy that you finally have a reason to wear my hat, scarf, and gloves."

Tracy narrowed her eyebrows. "It's not the weather I don't like! It's everyone wearing winter clothes to school that I have a problem with!"

"Why?" I asked and smiled.

"Why do you think I wear this hat, the scarf, and the gloves?"

I shrugged. "Enlighten me."

"Because I want to look different from everyone! If I wanted to look like everyone else, I would go to a school with mandatory uniforms!"

I burst out laughing.

Tracy shook her head. "This is not funny. If this weather doesn't change soon, they all will buy their own hats, scarves, and gloves!"

"Yes, that would be an injustice. I don't think you would like living up North with blizzards, girl," I said.

"Of course not. I'm an island girl," Tracy replied and smiled.

I leaned against the palm tree and closed my eyes, enjoying the chilly wind on my face.

I thought about my previous town, where temperatures dropped below freezing, where people looked forward to days like this one.

But soon, my daydreaming ended when something heavy fell on my stomach. I felt pain and opened my eyes immediately.

IT WAS AN IGUANA!

I don't know if you have ever seen an iguana, but they look like small dragons!

Instantly, Tracy and I screamed at the top of our lungs.

All the kids rushed toward us to see what was going on.

When I shoved the creature off my stomach and got up, we noticed the iguana didn't move.

"It's dead," I said. "Did I kill it?"

"It's not dead," I heard Alex say behind me. "It's frozen. Iguanas are cold-blooded reptiles, and they need warm temperatures to function. That's why they bask in the sun all day. The cold weather paralyzes them, and they fall from the trees."

"Will the iguana survive?" I asked him.

"Yes. When it gets warmer, its blood will thaw, and the iguana will wake up. But we can speed up the process by bringing it inside the school and covering it with something warm."

"Let's do it," other kids started saying.

So, Alex picked up the reptile, and we followed him inside the building. He placed the animal in an empty tank in the science classroom, and he covered it with his sweater.

When the bell rang, nobody wanted to leave the new school pet, so the teachers let us stay and watch over the reptile for the rest of the afternoon.

And when the iguana's body warmed up, we saw it move its jaws a little. Then it slowly started moving its whole body.

Everyone clapped when we saw the iguana get up, trying to escape.

Mrs. Clark said it was too cold to let it go outside because it would freeze again. So, everyone was happy to hear that our new school pet could stay with us for a few more days.

After putting food and water in the tank, everyone agreed we should name him.

"Godzilla!" one boy said.

"Dragon," someone else suggested.

Alex shook his head. "I think Sylvia should choose since she is the one who found it."

The iguana dropped on top of me, but . . . I guess it's close enough.

I thought for a few seconds, then said, "Spikey, for the spikes on its back."

Everyone liked the name, so Spikey became our temporary pet until it warms up outside.

FRIDAY

Surprisingly, the weather warmed up overnight, but everyone at school seemed to be upset about it.

The only person happy about the heat was Tracy, who loved that she was once again the only kid at school in a hat and gloves, with a scarf around her neck.

Everyone else worried we would need to let Spikey go, but Mrs. Clark said that iguanas are invasive in the wild, so it would be okay for the school to keep Spikey as our school pet.

All the kids cheered to hear the great news, and everyone catered to the animal all day long.

I guess it's better to have an iguana than no pet at all.

This evening, we arrived at Grandma's, planning to stay until Sunday afternoon.

Grandma lives on a different island nearby, in a little cottage with a big fenced-in backyard and a large garden.

Natalia and I love visiting Grandma because she has a barn and a coop with hens.

I don't know why, but people in the islands LOVE having chickens, just like people in the country.

You can spot roosters and hens wandering down the streets everywhere, and you are lucky if crowing roosters don't wake you up in the early morning.

Our favorite thing to do at Grandma's is playing hide-and-seek and chasing each other around her barn.

Unfortunately, the chickens often get in our way, running away from us, flapping their wings.

Sometimes, I run into the coop so fast that I can't stop myself quickly, and I end up crashing into the eggs inside.

YUCK!!

The nasty smell from the chicken droppings and the smashed yolks make me want to puke!

Then I need a shower, so sometimes I think this whole chase isn't worth it.

But today, the whole yolk mess got me thinking.

How come when I smash the eggs in the coop, no chicklets ever come out of the eggs?

I must have missed some biology lessons because I seriously don't know.

That, of course, doesn't surprise me because I hardly ever paid any attention at my previous school, and I rarely tried to remember any facts.

But it wasn't all my fault!

I've always had a hard time focusing at school because of all the jerks judging me, waiting for me to mispronounce something or mix up some facts or trip in front of the entire class.

They watch you like hawks, ready for the kill.

Like vultures circling above, they'll watch you bleed to death, only so they can attack.

And by an attack, I mean excruciating LAUGHTER, teasing, and harassing.

Anyway, I decided to investigate this egg phenomenon. (**Phenomenon** is what adults call something they can't figure out.)

So, I quickly figured out there is no chance a chick will survive if we put a freshly laid egg in the refrigerator.

But what if we don't?

Since Grandma won't allow the hens to sit on the eggs for long, I decided to steal one egg and keep it warm myself.

It took a while to find a perfect spot for the nest, but in the end, I put it under the pillow on the bed where I was sleeping at Grandma's.

Grandma has those old-fashioned pillows with real feathers, so this would really make the little chicklet feel like his momma was sitting on him.

I'M GLAD HUMANS DON'T DO THAT! CAN YOU IMAGINE? YUCK!!

Of course, I kept my secret from my sister, which I soon regretted.

You see, sometimes I should include that little kid in my plans because keeping her in the dark just backfires on me all the time.

I spent an entire evening catering to that egg under my pillow. I made sure it was warm and safe. I talked to it. I even sang it a song.

I thought about keeping the chicklet as my pet and seeing it grow. Having Spikey in our classroom made me crave my own pet for sure!

But Natalia knew nothing about it, so she used that one minute I was in the bathroom to crash on my bed with all her toys!

"NOOOOO!!" I screamed and ran to save the baby chick!

But it was too late! The yolk was all over my sheet.

😮

Natalia is used to me getting mad at her when she touches my stuff, but I must have really scared her this time.

"You killed the baby chick!" I said.

She looked at me with panic in her eyes. "I didn't do anything! I swear!"

But there was no point talking to her. That little chicklet's life was gone forever.

😫

I showed her the mess under my pillow and told her I was trying to hatch a baby chick.

As soon as she saw the evidence of murder, she cried hysterically.

Mom rushed into the room. "What happened? Who is hurt?"

Mom always thinks the worst!

I explained to her what had happened and how Natalia killed the baby chick.

Mom smiled and asked my sister to stop crying. "There was no chicklet inside that egg, honey."

I sighed. "Not yet, but I was trying to hatch it." Duh!

"An egg needs to be fertilized first to become a chicken," Mom said. "Grandma doesn't allow fertilization, so we can eat the eggs and not worry about baby chicks."

Natalia wiped her tears. "So, all Sylvia was missing was a fertilizer?"

Mom laughed. "Only roosters can fertilize the eggs. If Grandma had roosters, chances are those eggs could have little chicklets in them if the hens kept them warm long enough."

"But how can hens lay eggs without the rooster?" Natalia asked.

"Hens will lay eggs whether or not a rooster is around. Only when a hen mates with a rooster are the eggs fertilized, which means little chicklets can hatch from them if kept warm for some time. Without the rooster, hens lay unfertilized eggs, the same eggs we buy in the stores."

I sighed. "So, no chicklet was in my egg. . . ."

Mom shook her head. "No, honey."

Mom's words made Natalia feel better. I could tell she was glad she hadn't actually crushed a baby chick.

I must admit, I feel better, too.

I smooshed so many eggs in that coop that the guilt of possibly destroying future chickens haunted me in my nightmares many times.

Now I can sleep well—for as long as no rooster ever enters Grandma's property.

SATURDAY

While still at Grandma's, I decided to put my MIDDLE SCHOOL GOAL into action and earn some extra cash for my future plan!

So, I thought it would be a good idea to start a new business and sell eggs to all of Grandma's neighbors.

Like, an **EGG**cellent idea!

I knew freshly laid, unwashed eggs didn't have to be refrigerated for days, so I wasn't worried about them getting spoiled.

This time, I included my sister in my plan.

Grandma always complains we get in too much trouble when we are together, but I think that's just a given.

We took Grandma's wagon from the shed behind the house, and we laid all the eggs on a blanket inside.

I didn't think it would be a problem for Grandma since the hens lay eggs for her every day.

We snuck out of the yard unnoticed and headed down the road.

"This is so exciting!" my sister said. "How much money do you think we can earn?"

I shrugged. "I don't know. How much do eggs cost at stores? We should charge more because we actually DELIVER them to people's houses."

"Fifty cents each?" she asked.

"More like a dollar each!" I said.

We both nodded and rolled the wagon to our first house.

I knocked and waited for someone to open the door. An old man answered.

"Good morning, sir. We're selling eggs, so this is your lucky day because you won't have to go to the store today," I said.

The old man shook his head. "I don't need any eggs. I have my own chickens."

Well, we didn't think about this!

Does everyone in the islands have their own chickens? We definitely don't, and I know Mom is not planning to have any!

We knocked on several houses, but the people who lived in them turned us away. They all had chickens!

We were a little bummed after this because we both really could use some cash.

Natalia is saving for a new bike, and I have my MIDDLE SCHOOL PLAN to worry about.

I don't know what happened to Santa Claus this year, but neither of us got what we wanted for Christmas. I wanted a dog, but of course, that didn't happen!

Maybe Grandma is right—we must get in trouble too much.

Anyway, when I realized a farmer's market was near the church in town, I immediately suggested going there to make the sales.

My sister agreed, so off we went.

When we got there, we set up our station.

There wasn't that much to do, honestly. We positioned the wagon in front of us and waited for people to line up to buy eggs from us.

The only problem was nobody did! There was no interest from anyone!

Why weren't they buying the eggs?

Natalia suggested we start waving and dancing to attract everyone's attention, just like those inflatable creatures some businesses use on the streets.

As soon as we started goofing around, a few people came to our station.

But they weren't happy with the one-dollar-per-egg price tag, so they left.

We were stunned because we truly believed that removing an egg from a coop and hauling it to a farmer's market was surely worth a buck, but I guess adults have little value for child labor.

The next person who came to us was a tall man with a cowboy hat. "I can buy a dozen eggs for six dollars from you."

WHAT? Six dollars?? For twelve eggs?? That's an outrage!

He noticed my shocked face and added, "That's more than they cost in the store."

Huh? If twelve eggs cost so little, then I don't know how people make any money around here!

We were definitely NOT HAPPY about this deal, but we agreed to sell them to him since we were running out of time.

Farmer's markets close very early.

By the time we sold all twenty-four eggs for "the going rate of six dollars per dozen (!)," we earned twelve dollars together.

When we divided it among the two of us, we each ended up with six dollars, which was a total waste of time, in my opinion.

The person selling baskets near our station saw us counting our money and told us we should be happy with what we had received.

She said we were lucky we were not caught by an officer checking whether we had paid for our spot in the farmer's market.

Apparently, people need to pay the market's owner for selling their things there, which doesn't make any sense to me.

And just like that, we saw an officer walking toward us.

It took us only a second to grab the wagon and run.

When the man started chasing us, we sprinted between the sellers' stands, hoping he would lose sight of us.

But he knew the market pretty well because he was ahead of us every time. We had to back up and run in the opposite direction to escape from him.

I wasn't ready to go to jail before I even reached middle school, and I definitely didn't want to end up on the front-page news, either.

I don't mind publicity, but smuggling eggs is not what I would call foot-in-the-door fame.

I realized we had to do something creative to lose the guy, so I directed us toward a stand with clothes, and we hid between the racks with island dresses.

My plan worked—the officer passed by without noticing us at all.

When he disappeared from our view, we quickly left so nobody could take away whatever money we had.

We hauled the empty wagon back to Grandma's house, vowing never to sell eggs again.

Along the way, we decided to prolong our schooling years until we were thirty because, apparently, the adult world isn't all it's cracked up to be.

SUNDAY
GREAT! JUST GREAT!

You won't believe what happened to me today!

We were still at Grandma's this morning, but things were quite slow, so I soon became bored.

Mom, Dad, and Grandma sat on sofas in the living room and talked while Natalia painted at the dining room table.

I was in the guest room, trying to occupy myself, which wasn't working out.

Then, I overheard Grandma saying how recently she had been suffering from memory loss, and to be honest with you, it wasn't news to me.

I thought she had been dealing with it for quite some time because she had been telling us the same stories over and over again for years now.

Mom told Grandma nothing was wrong with her because Mom would surely notice if something was.

So, obviously, Mom must have been zoning out during Grandma's stories, but I figured it was best not to say anything.

Grandma said she swore she had many eggs in the coop yesterday morning, but they all were gone by noon.

She wanted to bake us a cake and make scrambled eggs this morning, but the coop was empty.

As soon as we heard it, Natalia and I looked at each other and smiled, but we both kept quiet.

Their conversation gave me an idea to trick my family with another prank and have some fun.

I love pranking people! Especially my sister.

But to prank the whole family? It was an exciting challenge!

My plan was to confuse Grandma even more.

I know . . . I know . . . You don't have to tell me! But I can't stop myself. If I don't prank someone from time to time, my mind goes insane!

I told my sister to join me in the guest room. When we were finally alone, I told her about my plan. "If I let them know I am in the house, but then I keep coming in from outside, they won't figure out how I am doing it."

My sister giggled, excited for another prank.

I walked into the kitchen, making sure everyone noticed me, then I returned to the guest room.

I opened a window in the guest room, moved the plants in the clay pots aside, and climbed outside.

The house was only one story, so I jumped and safely landed on the ground.

I walked to the front door and entered the house.

I passed everyone in the living room back to the guest room.

I giggled when I heard Grandma talking.

"You see! I swear I saw Sylvia in the house a few minutes ago, yet she just came from outside," she said to Mom. "My mind doesn't work the way it used to."

I didn't hear how Mom responded because I was climbing out the window again.

When I entered the house the second time, everyone looked at me, confused.

"Honey," Mom asked, "when did you leave the house?"

I shrugged. "I don't know. Some time ago."

"Hmm . . ." Mom said and looked at Dad.

I withdrew to the guest room and laughed.

I waited five minutes to see if any of them would follow me, then I climbed through the window again.

When I entered the house the third time, Grandma put a hand on her head. "I'm losing my mind."

Mom and Dad looked at each other with concern.

"I could swear she was just here," Mom said. "Natalia, did you see Sylvia leave?"

"Yes, I did," my sister said and smiled. But nobody asked her HOW I left.

Only Dad stared at me with suspicion.

I calculated I had about one more run before he discovered how I did it.

I went to the guest room and waited. Suddenly, Natalia barged into the room. "They are coming to check on you. Get out now! I will close the window behind you," she said.

I hurried toward the window and started climbing through it again. I could already imagine their shocked faces when they discovered I was NOT in the room.

But my body must have been growing tired because I lost my balance, and no matter what I tried to grab on to, I landed on the ground . . . right on my wrist.

I heard a loud noise of pots breaking around me, and all I felt was excruciating pain.

The entire family rushed to me.

"What happened?" Mom asked, hovering over me.

"Honey, are you okay?" Dad said and tried to pick me up.

I screamed. The pain was too much to bear.

Dad looked at my swollen wrist. "It looks like it's broken. We need to take her to the hospital."

"Sylvia, what were you doing?" Grandma asked.

"Climbing through the window," I said, although I could hardly speak.

"But why?" she asked.

I shrugged. "I don't know why kids do things. We just do."

"Well, you, young lady, will explain this behavior later," Mom said, "after we return from the hospital."

Then Mom turned to Grandma. "You see, your mind is working just fine. Sylvia was just leaving the house through your window, so we couldn't see her exit the house."

Grandma eyed her, confused. "But how do you explain the missing eggs?"

"We sold them," I confessed because everyone's attention was stirring away from the real tragedy here—my broken wrist.

I told them the whole truth—how people ripped us off with low prices and how we practically made no money after the entire day's work.

Grandma was really mad because we gave away all her eggs, and I ruined all her pots and plants near the window.

Mom was upset, too. "I can't believe you were climbing through a window! You will be in middle school soon!"

There it was—the MIDDLE SCHOOL words again. People expect you to change overnight miraculously, and then they wonder why kids dread it.

MIDDLE SCHOOL

WHAT IF I'M NOT
READY TO GROW UP?

The only person who thought today was a good lesson in the real world was Dad, but him being on my side didn't help me much.

Mom made me pay for all the pots and plants with my own savings and the money I had earned the day before, so basically, the entire weekend was a waste.

MONDAY
I have a broken wrist, all right!

The doctor at the hospital put a cast on my entire arm, bent at the elbow and held in place by a special scarf.

Although Mom is upset because I can't get it wet for the next three weeks and take normal showers, I am thrilled for an entirely different reason:

NO MORE PE
FOR THREE WEEKS!

I finally have a perfect excuse to sit back, chill, and do absolutely nothing!

I may even fake soreness for a few more weeks and possibly skip PE for much longer.

Maybe I can even take off from school for three weeks!

I'm already imagining new strategies for winning the BUILDING WORLDS game against my online friends.

With all that extra free time, I can stay ahead of everyone.

But Mom has different plans for me.

She is frustrated because she needs to wrap my arm in plastic bags before I shower, and since I can't use the other hand, it takes me forever to wash.

And getting dressed takes unique skills, too, so by the time I'm ready for the day, Mom loses over two hours helping me.

Today, I told her I shouldn't have to go to school at all because my hand was in the cast.

But she said I broke my right wrist, and I write with my left hand.

She added that if I could play on my tablet, I could write and study, too.

I tried explaining that writing is more difficult than touching a screen, but that just backfired on me.

Although I was allowed to stay home today, I will be returning to school tomorrow.

Mom says I need to go to PE classes, too, and I will just walk in circles around the field because my legs are perfectly fine!

ARE YOU KIDDING ME? CAN'T A PERSON GET A BREAK AROUND HERE?

Well, I'm not gonna give up the fight that easily!

TUESDAY

This morning, on the day of PE, I lay in bed, making sounds as if I were in pain.

I was fine, but faking an illness would surely get me out of going to school and doing sports.

And I was right. As soon as Mom realized my wrist still hurt, she said I could stay home for a few extra days.

"But if you stay home, then you can't go to the Winter Dance on Saturday."

"I wasn't planning to go to the Winter Dance, so that's fine with me."

"But Natalia won't be able to go, either, because kids up to second grade need to be accompanied by their parents. Unfortunately, Dad will be away this weekend, Grandma has an event to go to, and I can't leave you home alone."

I couldn't believe my luck!

No PE this week, a few days off—away from Brittany!—and I'm forced to stay home during the Winter Dance?

THIS BROKEN WRIST TURNED OUT TO BE THE BEST THING EVER!

I was thrilled I scored this time, but Natalia started crying immediately.

She said it was unfair that she had to stay home while all she wanted was to have fun with the kids from the island school.

"Why do you always have to ruin everything for me? Why can't you be happy around other kids?" Natalia screamed into my face and ran to her room.

Why can't she be happy just being home?

She has me, after all.

I can be fun to be around, too!

Right?

After Natalia returned from school, she didn't want to speak to me and avoided me at all times.

Only before bed, she came to my room and said, "I know you are faking it just to stay home."

I didn't manage to respond because she quickly added, "I don't want to be friends with you anymore!"

Am I really such a horrible sister?

WEDNESDAY

Today, I decided to show my sister I am a fun companion, too, and she doesn't need to look for kids somewhere else.

When Natalia returned from school, I walked into her room, plopped myself on the carpet, and said, "Let's play . . ."

Natalia looked at me as if I'd just come from Mars. "You don't know how to play."

"I'm sure I remember how to do it. What do you want to play?"

Natalia opened her toy bin and removed tons of dolls, little dresses, and tiny shoes.

"You can be Lola, and I'll be Flora," she said and handed me one doll.

Okay, I thought, I can do this.

But Natalia kept telling me to do this and do that, say this, answer that—I could hardly catch up.

Man, if she bosses all the kids like that, I feel sorry for them already.

After twenty minutes of playing with my sister, my head hurt, and I no longer had to pretend I was in pain.

So, I put Lola in her bed, covered her with a blanket, and said, "Lola needs a nap now."

I grabbed my tablet and turned on my BUILDING WORLDS game.

Natalia was upset I didn't want to play with her anymore and ran to Mom to complain I was online all day long.

As you can see, little kids rarely appreciate what older siblings do for them!

Besides, it's not my fault I'm too old to play with dolls!

Mom told me to get off the tablet and go outside, but I quickly reminded her that with a broken wrist, I couldn't bike, use my scooter, swim in the pool, or jump on the trampoline.

When I told her I was practically forced to be online all day long, she didn't want to hear it.

Mom said if I already felt better playing on my tablet, then I was ready to go back to school, too!

End of conversation.

THURSDAY

This morning, I faked pain again, so Mom said I could stay home for the rest of the week, which means we are definitely NOT going to the Winter Dance at school.

Natalia is still mad at me for "ruining her life," so she hardly speaks to me.

After another day of her silent treatment and four days away from school, I'm starting to forget what my voice sounds like, and I really worry I will forget how to talk.

I read somewhere that if you don't use your muscles every day, you will lose them.

This is why people who spend their days doing nothing all day long have flabby arms and difficulties walking.

So, this afternoon, I decided to chat with Tracy online to see each other and exercise my vocal cords with her.

"What happened? What were you doing?" she asked when I told her about my broken wrist.

"Climbing through the window."

She looked at me, puzzled. "Please, do explain. I really hope there is a good story behind it."

"Not really," I said and told her about my prank.

She cringed. "You could have ruined your clothes, you know!"

I burst out laughing. "Yes. That would be worse than breaking my wrist. A TRAGEDY!"

Tracy adjusted the winter hat on her head, still wearing my gloves and the scarf I'd given to her.

"I don't understand why this is funny for you. I think when you are about to start middle school, you worry about your looks," she said.

"We won't start middle school until September," I pointed out.

"Well, then you have eight months to grow up," she said and laughed.

"Very funny," I said and smiled.

Tracy sighed. "You poor thing! Now you can't do anything!"

"Who said I wanted to do something?" I asked.

"But what about the Winter Dance? You can't miss that!"

"I hate dresses, and I don't want to go with a cast on my hand."

"Sylvia, please, think about it. It will be fun!"

"I doubt it," I said. "Besides, Mom says I can't go because I missed the entire week of school, being in pain."

"Were you in pain?"

"No, but I don't think she will believe me that I miraculously healed for the dance."

"All girls in the world miraculously heal for a dance party. She will understand."

"Tracy, I would look ridiculous in a dress and a cast! Even if I had a dress, which I don't."

"I can lend you one—"

"No, thanks. Tell me, how is Spikey doing in the classroom?"

"Everyone fights over who will feed the iguana each day. It's hilarious."

"I'm glad, but I need to go. Mom's calling me for dinner. Good night, Tracy," I said and ended the video call.

It was nice talking to Tracy, but I'm sure brief conversations with her won't be enough to help me keep my voice, though.

So, now I realize my existence depends on talking to my sister, and I know I have to make peace with her as soon as possible.

☺☺

And that means—going to the dreaded Winter Dance so she can meet with her friends! Ugh!

FRIDAY

When my sister returned from school, I walked into her room, where she was playing with dolls by herself, and I sat down beside her.

"I'm sorry I was such a grump. I may be a loner, but that doesn't mean you shouldn't meet with other kids because of me. We can go to the Winter Dance tomorrow if Mom lets me go."

"Forget it. I'm not going!" Natalia responded.

"YOU'RE NOT GOING?" I asked in disbelief.

She shook her head. "You were right. This school is stupid! We should be homeschooled!"

I sat near her on the bed. "What happened?"

"I got into a fight," she said.

"A FIGHT?" I repeated, stunned.

My sister with perfect behavior and tons of award stickers?

"With whom?"

"Max Gunov! The meanest kid in second grade."

Natalia said I missed all the drama this week at school, so she told me the entire story.

Max Gunov is in her class, and he is always in trouble. Teachers pull their hair out trying to teach while he goofs around all the time.

He loves calling the kids all kinds of names, tripping them in the hallways, and stealing their things.

He threatens boys after school and fights with many terrified second graders.

But what is even worse, he is awfully mean to girls!

As you may suspect, Natalia wasn't going to fear him in front of everyone, and she decided to put a stop to his bullying.

Mom had given me and Natalia cell phones to reach her in case of emergency. She also uses them as tracking devices, so she always knows where we are.

Not a big deal—many kids bring cell phones to school.

This week, every time Natalia heard Max call the kids mean names or saw him pushing someone, she recorded him on her cell phone.

Once she collected enough evidence, she showed the videos to Max and told him to stop the bullying, or she would show the recordings to their teacher, Mrs. Jones.

Max was furious and called Natalia all kinds of names on the school playground during recess, where all the kids could hear.

Although Natalia couldn't stop tears from rolling down her cheeks, she was smart to record the whole thing on her cell phone.

When she showed the videos to the teacher, Mrs. Jones made Max apologize to Natalia and all the kids he had bullied before, and she took away his recess until the end of the week.

I'm sure the teacher called his parents as well, and they probably grounded him for some time.

HE DESERVED IT!

But, of course, their confrontation didn't end there.

Max was so mad he had missed recess for many days that as soon as he could join their class outside today, he pushed Natalia in front of the swings.

This time, Natalia defended herself, and they got into a fight.

LIKE A REAL FIGHT!

Natalia wanted to free herself from Max's arms, so she bit his hand—hard.

She told me that Max screamed like a baby!

By the time teachers came, it looked like Natalia was the one who had started it all.

"Mrs. Jones reprimanded me in front of the entire class!" Natalia said, tears streaming down her cheeks. "I never want to go back to this school again!"

When Natalia told me what had happened, I made a mental note to myself NOT TO EVER get into a physical fight with my sister. When Natalia saw Max's hand, she told me it looked pretty serious.

I wasn't that surprised, though, because I remembered how Natalia had bitten some other kid's nose when she was only two in daycare. It had something to do with a stolen cracker.

So, now that I know her biting is a reoccurring tendency, I'll make sure I stay away when we argue.

"Cool!" I said when I realized that, for the first time, my stealing-all-my-things sister did something totally awesome!

In the end, I must have taught her well.

"So, you really don't want to go to the Winter Dance tomorrow?" I asked Natalia.

She shook her head. "Never in a million years!"

Okay, I admit I felt relieved when my sister told me she didn't want to go to that dance.

There are many reasons why I have been dreading this event, hoping I would never have to go there:

1. Since all classes are invited—elementary and middle school—I will have to face TONS of unfamiliar faces, all in one night! No, thank you!

2. DANCE = DRESSES, and I would rather be caught dead than wearing a dress! Not that I have any in my closet.

3. Even if I put on a dress, I don't think my combat boots would look good with it. And I don't own any other shoes besides sneakers. Neither would I want to.

4. A TOMBOY in a dress, surrounded by tons of strangers, is already a scary scenario, but a tomboy in a dress with her hand in a cast is just a laughable joke!

5. All that just mentioned will surely give Brittany a GREAT reason to turn me into the Winter Dance CLOWN—the entertainment of the year.

No, thank you!

So, yes, I admit I was happy that my sister knew what it was like to be ME for the first time!

But then . . .

. . . I started thinking . . .

That . . .

If my sister—the one who fears no one—starts avoiding kids the way I do, then people like me have no chance of ever making friends with ease at all.

If I don't help Natalia get back on the horse (as Mom calls it), all the introverts in the world will be doomed for life.

So . . . I had to do what needed to be done.

"Come on," I told Natalia. "We're going to buy dresses for the Winter Dance because there's no way you are missing it."

"I told you—I don't want to go," she said.

"If you stay home, you will let Max Gunov win. And you don't like to lose."

"So what? I don't care if he wins. I'm not going back to that school ever again."

"If YOU don't stand up to him, no other kid will. He will bully all your friends because you decided to quit. After all, he always wins, right?"

Natalia sighed but said nothing.

"You need to walk onto that dance floor like you own the place," I continued. "All your friends will be ecstatic to see you. And you will show them that NOTHING will bring you down."

"What about you?" she asked. "You don't want to go."

"I will go if you go. And hey, if Max Gunov gives you any trouble, he will have to deal with me and my CAST. I'll use it as our shield to protect you."

Natalia burst out laughing, then gave me a huge hug.

Ugh, I'm not big on hugs; have I mentioned that?

Mom was happy I did the right thing and was willing to go, so she drove us to the local store to buy fancy dresses right away.

With only one clothing store on the island, I really hoped that all the girls at our school ordered their dresses from some fancy magazines weeks in advance— otherwise, we would all wear the same outfits.

So much for choices!

☹

"Sylvia," Mom said on the way to the store, "you don't even know how much it means to me that you are finally ready to open up and have fun with your friends from school."

"I'm only doing it for my sister," I said.

But deep inside, I was looking forward to seeing Alex and Tracy.

No matter how ridiculous I will look.

SATURDAY

When Natalia and I entered the school cafeteria where the Winter Dance took place, we looked like Ghostbusters, ready to face the enemies.

The fog rose behind us as the bright lights shone in our direction, making it the best entrance of my life.

Or so I imagined.

I wore a black dress that wasn't as terrible as I had thought and boots that were more feminine and elegant than those I usually wear.

I wouldn't win a beauty contest, but I looked all right. The best that was possible.

On the other hand, my sister rocked with her shimmering dress that looked as if it was made of glitter.

When we entered, all eyes were on us, and it felt so good to attract everyone's attention for once.

Tracy wasn't kidding when she said they were celebrating winter.

Cool blue light lit the whole place. Paper snowmen and snowflakes hung from the ceiling. And fake snow blew in the corner.

Could this be the only way some kids experience "true" winter?

When Natalia showed me Max Gunov, he stared at my sister, speechless.

When we approached him together, I tried to look and sound like I meant business, although I could hardly breathe. I had never even tried to stand up for myself, let alone someone else!

"Hey, Max," I said. "We have a problem. You see, I'm Natalia's older sister. . . . And as an older sister, I need to protect her." I raised my cast just a tiny bit so he would notice it. "You can understand that, right?"

With his eyes wide open, he stared at the cast, then right at me.

When he nodded, I continued, "So, you understand that when you bully her, you attack me, too, right?"

He swallowed hard and nodded.

"Good. That's all I wanted you to know."

Natalia smiled at me, gave Max a killer glance, and joined her friends on the dance floor.

I could feel Max's stare as I was walking away, happy not to be afraid anymore.

"OMG!" Tracy said as soon as she saw me. Apart from her cute dress, she wore all the winter stuff I'd given to her—the hat, the scarf, the gloves, and the long boots she wanted. "There is hope for you! You look so different!"

I smiled. "Good different or bad different?"

"The best different!" she said, then made a sad face when she finally noticed my cast. "Wow! That looks like it hurt!"

I laughed, but then I noticed her curls were gone. "What happened to your hair?"

Her hair was straight but all frizzy, as if she were electrocuted or something. Thank goodness she had my winter hat on her head.

"I look like a burned witch when I straighten my hair!" she said. "How am I ever gonna look different?"

"I think you are fine the way you are."

"Thanks, but I will come up with a way to look different for middle school."

I smiled, then looked around the dance floor. In the back of the cafeteria, I spotted Spikey in his glass tank.

We both walked up to the iguana. "Hey, buddy. I'm glad you are doing well," I said and patted him on his back.

Then my eyes searched for Alex.

"He's over there." Tracy pointed to a group of boys talking in the corner. "Do you think the two of you will exchange more than three sentences today?"

"You know I'm too shy to talk to him."

Tracy sighed. "I just wish all those boys standing against the walls knew they don't have to support the walls at all. The building won't collapse if they go dancing."

I laughed while I silently prayed NOBODY would ask me to dance.

Alex must have sensed we were talking about him because he looked at me . . . and I recognized a shock on his face.

Oh no, he hated the way I looked!

I knew I should have never come to this stupid dance!

He approached me. "What happened to you?"

I looked down. "I know. I look ridiculous in this dress."

When I looked up, he was staring at me, puzzled.

"I have never seen anyone look more beautiful IN A DRESS than you. . . ."

My cheeks were burning like a blazing fire. "Um . . . thanks."

"What happened to your hand? That's what I wanted to know."

"Oh, don't ask. I'm ashamed to even talk about it."

Wait? What? Since when was I ashamed of my pranks?

"That's a really cool cast," he told me.

"Thanks."

"Do you want to dance?"

No! I didn't want to dance! I didn't know how! I feared I would step on him, and he would end up with his toes in a cast next.

Can you imagine?

But I nodded and let him direct me to the dance floor.

This was not how you would imagine the first dance with a boy.

There was definitely something between us.

Unfortunately, THAT SOMETHING was my CAST!

Forget about comfortably putting my hands on his shoulders. The cast kept a larger space between us than an overprotective parent would!

But I finally gathered the courage to ask him if he was the one who left the sweets on my table during the geography fair.

"Did you like them?" he replied and smiled. "I thought some of them were awful."

I giggled. "True. But most of them were delicious. So, thank you."

"Glad I sweetened your day," he said and smiled. "Can I be the first to sign your cast?"

"Of course."

As soon as the slow music ended, he grabbed my other hand and led me to his circle of friends.

"Graffiti time!" he said and took out a marker from his pocket.

All his friends complimented me on the cast and started drawing all over it, too.

Later, many other kids came over to me and asked if they could sign my cast.

I said sure, and within a minute, I had a large group of kids scribbling on the cast.

Some boys were drawing artistic graffiti, and I was impressed with their talent.

I kind of liked all the attention I was getting, so I told everyone they could sign my other hand, too.

They loved the idea, and soon, I was covered in colorful markings on my other arm and even both legs.

Everyone seemed to have a good time, except Brittany, who marched toward me, probably dissatisfied that I was stealing everybody's attention from her.

"Well, well, well . . . Look who managed to turn herself into a Cinderella," Brittany said with a smirk on her face. "Lucky for you, the party ends before midnight."

I expected to hear a burst of laughter from everyone around me—because honestly, I thought her comment was hilarious—but instead, they all screamed together:

"SHUT UP, BRITTANY!!"

I couldn't hide my smile at the happiness I felt inside.

But when I saw tears welling up in the corners of Brittany's eyes, I asked her if she wanted to sign my cast.

She hesitated for a moment, but then she must have realized that writing on my cast could put her in the center of everyone's attention again, so she nodded and took her time to draw her name.

BRITTANY

For the rest of the night, Natalia and I enjoyed the Winter Dance, surrounded by our new friends and having fun.

I giggled when I looked at the creative drawings all over my arms and legs—it seemed so edgy!—but Mom didn't share my excitement when she saw me after the dance.

She said it would take a lot of scrubbing to remove the ink from my body.

I told Mom we didn't have to remove anything from my skin because I liked the way everything looked, but Mom didn't want to hear it.

She was right—it was painful to scrub my body clean.

Before bed, I inspected my cast and noticed something I must have missed during the party.

A drawing of a heart with the words "I LIKE YOU" was scribbled inside.

I stared at that heart for a while, wondering who had drawn it, but something was telling me that I already knew. . . .

For the first time . . . maybe . . . I'm looking forward to going back to school on Monday and seeing everyone.

Especially that one boy . . . whose name is Alex.

SUNDAY

As soon as Sunday morning rolled around, I video called Tracy.

"I'm trying a new look," she said. "But my mom doesn't let me wear makeup yet! She's killing my chances to complete my plan."

"How about a new middle school goal?" I asked.

"No, I'm still not giving up! How is your plan going? Have you started earning any money?"

"Yes, but it didn't turn out the way I had planned," I said. "I'm still at square one with my MIDDLE SCHOOL GOAL."

Then I told her about the heart with "I LIKE YOU" inside it on my cast.

I showed it to her on the screen.

She looked at it and gasped. "You must be kidding me!" Tracy said. "How exciting!"

"Yeah, it's nice . . . but what do I do?" I asked.

"It's not just nice, it's AMAZING! Just go talk to him the next time you see him at school."

"Talk? Like . . . me and him . . . alone?"

"Yes, silly. You and him, alone, like normal kids do," she said and laughed.

Who said I was normal?

"That's easy for you to say—you have no anxiety around other kids. Me? I don't think I have ever spoken with a boy for more than a few minutes."

"You will be fine!"

"Okay . . . I will try to talk to him," I said.

Will I have enough courage, though?

Later, Natalia asked me what that MIDDLE SCHOOL GOAL was about. She had overheard me on the phone with Tracy talking about it.

Since we had just reconciled and started talking to each other again, I disregarded the fact she had been eavesdropping on my conversation.

"It's something you do to show you are more grown up since we will go to middle school in the fall. I decided to start earning money. That's what grown-ups do, right?"

She nodded. "Can I have a goal like that, too?"

"Nope, it's a middle school thing only," I said.

But, of course, my sister didn't listen to me. She ran to Mom and said she wanted to earn money, just like we did at Grandma's.

Mom didn't like that we went to the farmer's market selling eggs without adult supervision.

She told us we could get money by doing certain chores INSIDE the house instead of going to strangers.

She said it was great we had interests in building our own businesses, and she could use many of our services.

She said she would prepare a list of things that needed to be done at home, and we would get a weekly allowance if we did them.

I wasn't thrilled to have to do anything at home, as my time on my tablet was already limited. However, Natalia was excited about the idea, so I agreed to it, too.

But I wasn't looking forward to the dreaded chores!

Later, Mom taught us how to do our laundry. She showed us how to prepare our meals. We learned how to clean floors, vacuum carpets, and wash the tub and mirrors.

Basically, the deal is we are supposed to do things for ourselves and be responsible for our bathroom and rooms. Plus, we should do the dishes and clean the floor when Mom needs help.

Of course, we were supposed to do those chores in the past, too, but we always procrastinated and found excuses not to do them.

Mom says it will be hard for me to do chores with my hand in a cast, so I can start after the doctor removes it.

I wasn't complaining about that decision.

🙂

But I have to admit that I'm glad I finally know how to work our washing machine because Mom is horrible when it comes to laundry.

She hates folding clothes so much she avoids doing laundry as much as possible.

We basically wait until we run out of all our clothes and have no clean underwear, and only then is Mom motivated to wash our clothes.

And even when the clothes are clean, she often leaves them in a hamper, and we must dig through them to find the clothes we need.

So, now that I know how to do laundry, I can take care of my clothes, thank you very much.

🙂

Unfortunately, my first attempt at doing laundry didn't go as planned because Mom had forgotten to mention I shouldn't mix whites with colors.

I loaded the machine with all my white T-shirts, and I let Natalia put her dresses in with them.

And, of course, all my white clothes turned pink!

I thought I'd have a heart attack when I saw it.

But Natalia was excited because she knew I would never wear pink clothes, so she would get all my T-shirts now.

So, my first WASH was a WASH, and all the clothes went to my sister.

How is it that Natalia always seems to luck out?

Let's see how this allowance thing will go.

TUESDAY
My eleventh birthday is this weekend, but it's hard to be excited about it when you have to share one with your sister!

Yes! You heard me right!

Natalia and I have birthdays on the same day!

Can you imagine?

There are 365 days in a year, but she had to be born on MY BIRTHDAY! Go figure!

Since our birthdays are at the end of January, reverse back nine months, and that's May.

May 5th, to be exact!

CINCO DE MAYO!

Nobody from our family comes from Mexico, yet CINCO DE MAYO is the day when my parents apparently lose their heads!

It probably has something to do with the romantic fiestas they enjoy that day!

So, thanks to the Mexican people's victory over the French troops in 1862, Natalia and I were conceived!

THREE YEARS APART ON THE SAME DAY!

There is nothing more annoying than sharing your birthday with your sister, who is THREE YEARS younger than you!

Every year, the problem starts with one simple question our parents ask us:

"What do you girls want to do for your birthdays?"

So, Natalia and I have to agree on something we BOTH like to do!

Yeah, are you laughing already?

We tried to have joint birthday parties in the past, but that turned out to be a disaster for me every year.

I would invite the three or four people I could tolerate at school, completely happy to have a quiet and relaxing get-together.

But my sister would invite her entire classroom, which meant thirty little kids, screaming and running around, hogging my party!

NO, THANK YOU!

But that wasn't the worst of it!

Trying to agree on a party theme together was like pulling teeth! With your bare hands.

For me, the choice was always simple—a scary Halloween theme.

But my sister had to choose princesses, butterflies, and unicorns!

So, no wonder some parents of the kindergartners were not happy when they showed up at our party one year and saw half of the property was decorated with princess decorations, while the other half had skulls, skeletons, graves, vampires, and fake bloody bodies on the ground.

So, this year, Mom suggested we should just bring birthday cakes and snacks to the local park and enjoy a nice afternoon playing all kinds of games with the kids from our classrooms.

Mom says since I have my arm in a cast, I wouldn't be able to enjoy a pool party with a bounce house or a waterslide, so this is a perfect solution.

Natalia is always excited about being in the center of everyone's attention, so this suits her well.

Me? I'm not crazy about celebrating my birthday with a bunch of kids I hardly know, but . . . I would like to speak to Alex with no one around because he's been on my mind a lot lately, which is strange.

So, I agreed to Mom's plan, and today, I handed birthday invitations to all my classmates, including Brittany.

Mom says it's rude to single out one person from the class, and she told me to invite EVERYONE.

So, I did, but let me tell you—if she ruins my birthday party, I'm done being the nice girl!

Today, during PE, I thought I would have the courage to ask Alex about the heart on my cast, but Coach had him busy playing sports, and all I managed to do was quickly hand him my birthday invitation.

Since Coach excluded me from doing sports because of my cast, this was the best PE ever!

With all those kids invited to our party, I'm really
hoping I won't have knots in my stomach on my
birthday.

Wish me luck!

SATURDAY

Today is my and Natalia's birthday, so we started the
day with a celebratory breakfast with Mom and Dad in
the dining room.

Usually, we eat at the kitchen table, but when we have
people over or celebrate something, Mom decorates the
dining room table for the special occasion.

Mom fastened balloons to our chairs, and Dad prepared
pancakes with whipped cream, maple syrup, and
chocolate sprinkles.

Dad enjoys cooking more than Mom, and he is a great
chef.

Because Mom is always watching her diet, she lives on low-fat soups and salads with fish or chicken.

I'm glad we have Dad, who loves pasta, pancakes, and pizza, because I don't know how we would survive otherwise.

After a delicious, sugary breakfast, Mom and Dad sang at the table, "Happy birthday to you!"

"Thanks. . . ." I said and smiled.

"Can we open our presents?" Natalia asked, excited.

"Of course," Dad said and handed us two large, wrapped boxes.

We tore the things apart within seconds. "A fishing tackle and box!" Natalia screamed.

I got the same thing.

Dad smiled. "Now that we live in the islands, I thought we could start fishing together on the weekends."

"I want to, Daddy! I can catch big fish—I know I can!" Natalia screamed with joy.

"Thanks, that would be great," I said, although I wasn't sure whether I would even like fishing.

Dad handed us more gifts.

"My own fishing rod!" Natalia said. "I love it!"

I got a fishing rod as well.

"How about we go fishing after Sylvia's cast is removed?" Dad asked.

"Yay!" Natalia said and started organizing her tackle box with all the rubber lures and hooks inside it.

"Thanks, Mom, Dad . . . it's a nice present," I said.

I'm not sure I will enjoy fishing because I can't even imagine touching the slimy squid Dad usually puts on his hook.

The rubber lures may be okay, but you still have to watch the rod and wait for the fish.

It doesn't seem very exciting to me, but I'm willing to try.

Next, I surprised my sister with a present from me—a set of colorful, fluffy dresses. I had Mom order it online.

It wasn't that difficult to find them—all I had to do was search for clothes I WOULD NEVER WEAR myself, and that's how I knew they would be perfect for my sister.

Natalia screamed for joy when she saw the dresses. Then she pushed a box toward me.

"What's that?" I asked, surprised.

"A present for you from me, silly," she said.

When I opened the box, I couldn't believe my eyes! Inside was an ice machine to make snow cones!

"I love it! I've wanted one for a long time! Love it! Love it!" I said.

Later, we heard from Grandma on the phone, and we opened her birthday cards with checks she had sent us.

MONEY! $$$ MONEY! $$$ MONEY!

After breakfast, Dad loaded the car with snacks, food trays, our birthday cakes, and birthday decorations, and he drove us all to the park where our birthday party was scheduled.

We arrived early so we could decorate the pavilion near the playground.

Natalia chose a coral reef theme, so we decorated her side of the pavilion with aqua balloons, a tablecloth, and plates. We spread seashells on the table and hung paper sea stars.

I went with the Halloween theme, so my birthday decorations were black and dark purple. I hung a few skeletons around to set the scene.

We kept the food in large coolers so it wouldn't get spoiled while everyone played games.

As soon as everyone arrived, the kids were excited about the party.

To my surprise, even Brittany showed up. "You know," she said, "I only came to your birthday party because my parents canceled our weekend at a fancy resort last minute."

I smiled. "Great, I hope you'll have fun."

"I'll try. . . ."

I rolled my eyes, hoping my birthday would pass uneventfully.

Mom put the presents in the corner of the pavilion so we could open them after the cake.

I glanced around the crowd, searching for Alex, and I spotted him walking in my direction.

My heart fluttered, so I pretended I was busy setting up the table for my birthday party.

"Hey, birthday girl," he said as soon as he approached me.

"Hey," I said, looking away to hide my burning cheeks.

There was no way I could ever have a normal conversation with a boy. I just can't do it!

He stood there for a minute (although it felt like a lifetime), looking at me, then said, "Do you need my help?"

"Um . . ." It was too early to take out the food, and we had already hung all the decorations. "I think we're all done."

What could I possibly ask him to do?

He sighed. "Okay then . . . See you later?"

"Later," I responded and slowly exhaled.

I know I should have said something more meaningful to him. But I could hardly speak!

I'm such an awkward potato!

I was glad when Dad called everyone to join the game, and I was left alone for some time.

Because of my cast, Mom let me stay with her, and I helped her set the picnic tables and display the food.

After an hour, all the kids came to the pavilion, their cheeks red from running around.

Soon, everyone enjoyed the food, snacks, and cold drinks.

I thought I would be uncomfortable sitting around so many kids I hardly knew, but Alex sat near me, and I completely forgot to be nervous about everybody.

Instead, I was nervous about him!!

All I could think was that a BOY sat that close to me, and I could smell the shampoo in his hair, which reminded me of freshly washed linen.

After the meal, Mom and Dad cleared any empty plates and brought our birthday cakes.

Natalia's cake was decorated like a coral reef.

My cake looked like a graveyard.

Some things just don't change!

😄

"That's the coolest cake I've ever seen," Alex said.

I laughed. "I know, right?"

All the kids from my class agreed and circled the table to see it.

"Can I have the skeleton to eat?" someone asked.

"I want the coffin!"

"I'm eating the creepy gravestone for sure!"

"The zombie is mine!"

I laughed because it was funny to see everyone fight over my cake.

😄

Natalia had a circle of kids around her cake, too—little girls excited over mermaids and sparkly pearls in clamshells.

When Dad lit up the candles, Mom told us to make a wish. If we blew out the candles in one try, the wish would come true.

I pretended to think about it, but I already knew what I wanted—a new pack of TRUE friends from the island school. I wanted to know what it felt like to be LIKED.

I know it shouldn't be hard to achieve this, but we are talking about ME—a super shy and introverted person!

Finding a new friend is like a monumental step for me!

I know Tracy seems to like me now . . . But will our friendship last? Or will she ditch me as soon as she realizes how weird I am?

I don't know what Natalia's wish was, but we soon started blowing out candles.

 It was more like *trying* to blow them out because the candles remained lit, no matter how much we blew.

I worried my wish would never come true, so I repeatedly blew and blew and blew, but nothing happened—the flames kept coming back.

Kids laughed, so I blew even stronger.

Unfortunately, I didn't notice how much I was spitting on the cake until someone commented, "Maybe we shouldn't eat the cake anymore. . . ."

I felt tears welling up in the corners of my eyes. This was a nightmare! I had ruined a completely perfect cake!

I looked at puzzled Natalia, who had the same problem.

"Um . . . girls," Mom said, "I think I might have bought those prank relighting candles by accident, and you can't blow them out. . . ."

"MOM!!" Natalia and I screamed.

What if my birthday wish will never come true now?

All the kids continued to laugh while Mom removed the lit candles from the cakes and dumped them into a cup of water.

"Cake anyone?" Mom asked.

I saw kids thinking about all that spitting, and I held my breath. I ruined my cake!

"I'll have it," Alex said and handed his plate to my mom.

After him, all the kids lined up to get their portions and selected graveyard elements from the top.

I finally could breathe.

Maybe this party won't be a disaster, after all!

When everyone finished eating the cake, it was time to open the presents.

I received many art projects, sketchbooks, and paints, while Natalia got many teddy bears and girly outfits.

But you will never believe what Brittany had bought me! A PE outfit—a sporty T-shirt and shorts!

Are you kidding me?

"I just know how much you love sports," she said with a smirk on her face.

"Thanks," I replied, rolling my eyes.

But there was one present I was looking forward to opening—the one from Alex.

I unwrapped his gift carefully, and I gasped when I saw a book about haunted places around the world.

OMG! What a perfect present!

"I love it!" I exclaimed. "So cool!"

Alex smiled. "I'm glad you like it. I kind of thought you might enjoy it."

"I will! I love books like this! Thank you!"

He smiled, and this time it was his cheeks that were burning.

Then Tracy handed me a present—a set of large, blank canvases and an easel.

"This is so awesome! I will make my own paintings for my room! Thank you!" I said.

"I know how much you love art," she said.

Natalia and I thanked everyone for all the presents, then all the kids ran to the playground where Mom and Dad were waiting with all kinds of games to play.

Everyone left but Alex, and this was the moment I knew I had to talk to him.

Like, really TALK. . . .

But that was easier said than done because I have never been good with that kind of stuff.

It was awkward for me to look him in the eye, especially since I didn't know what to say to him.

But he made things easy for me because, as soon as I sat down on the bleachers, he plopped himself next to me and talked for fifteen minutes.

Because I didn't have to talk to him much, and he was okay with me just listening, I knew then I liked him, too.

Like a friend, of course.

He talked about his younger sister, Lily, who is Natalia's age. As far as he knew, Natalia and Lily had bonded already.

I told him about my previous school and what it was like to live up North during the chilly winter months.

After some time, I felt comfortable talking to him about anything.

"Were you the one who drew the heart on my cast?" I asked.

He nodded. "Yes, I'm happy you joined our school because you look like someone I would love to hang out with."

My face blushed immediately, but he didn't see it because Dad asked him to join everyone for another game.

I sat there for a few minutes, trying to gather my thoughts about all the recent changes in my life.

A new island life, a new home, a new school, a new group of kids who aren't trying to chew me up every time I speak, a boy who likes me . . .

Just a few months ago, I would have never imagined my life would turn for the better like this.

Eventually, even I joined the games—with my cast and all—and I had a great time!

I have to go now. Tracy is coming over for a birthday sleepover, and we have tons of things to talk about!

SUNDAY

OMG! The birthday sleepover was so much fun!

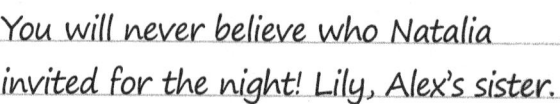

You will never believe who Natalia invited for the night! Lily, Alex's sister.

You can probably imagine my surprised face when I opened the door and saw Alex standing on the steps!

His mom and Lily were at the door, too, but all I could see was him.

A BOY! AT MY HOUSE!

Mom let them in, and while they were exchanging their phone numbers and discussing details of the sleepover plan, I showed my room to Alex.

I was thankful I had just finished cleaning it for my night with Tracy, who was on her way, because I didn't know what I would do if he saw the mess I sometimes have in my room.

Mom would say "sometimes" is an understatement, though.

"I like your room," Alex said, looking around.

"Thanks," I said.

I really love my room. I have a loft bed because I like to sleep on a higher elevation—this way, I never sleep close to dust balls and all the creepy things I lose, which always end up under the bed.

Below the loft bed, I have my desk and shelves filled with art supplies.

On the opposite side stands a bookcase full of my favorite comics. In the corner of the room, I have a comfortable sofa for lounging around.

"Would you like something to drink?" I asked, just to have a reason to leave and think for a moment.

When he nodded, I sprinted to our kitchen, and I could hardly breathe because a boy was in my room.

A BOY WAS IN MY ROOM!

With shaky hands (well, technically one since the other one is in the cast), I filled two glasses with a punch made from fresh fruits and returned to Alex.

"I love your emoji doodles," he said.

"Um . . . thanks!"

I have my emoji doodles on separate sheets of paper clipped to a rope that hangs against all four walls. The rope has tiny lights on it, giving a nice ambiance, which I love.

"You are really good with it. You should join our Art Club. We meet once a week after school and have tons of fun," he said, looking right at me.

My heartbeat accelerated. "I would love to! As soon as the doctor removes my cast, I would like to come."

"That's a good idea. You will need both of your hands to complete the projects we do there."

We talked for another ten minutes, and I laughed at his jokes, which was easy because they were hilarious.

We were both sitting on the sofa, sipping our drinks, when Tracy walked in.

You should have seen her surprised look! Like she saw a ghost who had just come to life!

And then a terror showed on her face because she must have realized she was wearing only . . . pajamas!

"Surprise!" I said, trying not to laugh.

She stood speechless at my door, so I raised myself and let her in.

Alex got up. "Um . . . I better go. You two enjoy your slumber party."

"Thanks for stopping by," I said.

"Pleasure was mine. And happy birthday again," he said and walked out of the room.

Tracy looked at me, clearly shocked that a male human was in my room.

I laughed. "I thought I was the shy one! You didn't even say hello."

"Would it kill you to inform me NOT to come in my pajamas because you planned to have a BOY over?"

I smiled. "I didn't plan for him to come over. He brought his sister to Natalia's sleepover."

Tracy plopped herself down on my sofa. "He's cute, isn't he?"

I sighed. "He's nice for sure."

Then I recapped my conversation with Alex.

"I'm glad the two of you finally spoke like good friends. I told you it wouldn't be that hard."

Later, Tracy, Lily, Natalia, and I hung out in the living room together because that's where all the snacks were.

Mom and Dad brought two small birthday cakes again, and this time, our candles blew out on the first try.

Maybe my birthday wish will come true—kids will like me, and I will have a pack of close friends at school.

When we were back in my room, Tracy and I watched an animated movie about vampires.

But when we finally went to bed—me in my bunk bed and Tracy on the pull-out sofa in my room—we both couldn't sleep.

Tracy told me she was scared after watching the movie (which was for kids, by the way!), so I told her to turn the side lamp on.

I could hardly sleep because my thoughts kept circling back to Alex.

I don't remember the last time a boy was so nice to me.

None of the boys at school even spoke to me.

But Alex let me know he wants to be my friend, and I'm getting excited to get to know him better.

Can I finally open up?

FEBRUARY

TUESDAY

Another week passed, so the doctor finally removed the cast yesterday, although I begged to keep it on for more time.

But Mom knew I just wanted to get out of doing sports during PE classes, so she wouldn't let me pull a fast one on her.

So today, during PE, I knew I would need to join everyone on the field.

As soon as I entered the school, many kids ran to me, happy to see me without the cast.

They checked my hand for any signs of total deterioration but were surprised by how nicely it healed.

Soon, Coach asked us to choose a teammate for a game that required two people to have one of their legs strapped together with another person's leg—something about learning how to work together and stuff.

Alex came over to me. "Are you in with me?"

I nodded. "Okay."

Again, I wasn't sure what we were playing, but Alex and I had fun running with our legs tied together. We laughed a lot!

Later, during recess, Alex and I decided to chill on the grass in the shade of a tree and talk.

Like, REALLY talk!

"So, how was your weekend?" Alex asked.

"It was great; I spent it mostly reading the book about haunted places you gave me for my birthday," I replied.

"What place was your favorite?"

"Florida! Do you know there is a museum in Key West where they have a haunted doll? They call it Robert the Doll! You can visit it, but people believe that if you take a photo of him, he will haunt you forever!"

"I've heard about him. It would be cool to see him."

"I know, right? The only problem is that many people who visit him send letters to the museum apologizing for taking his photos and begging Robert to let go of his curse on them! Apparently, many strange things happen to them after visiting Robert the Doll. I'm not sure I need that type of stress!"

Alex laughed. "You're funny. Would you visit a church that has walls decorated with human bones?"

"Yes! Does one like that exist?"

"In the Czech Republic, in a place called Kutná Hora, there is this Church of Bones where over 40,000 human skeletons are displayed in the chapel. They even made a chandelier from the bones."

"Really? But why?"

"Hundreds of years ago, many people wanted to be buried there because they believed its soil was holy. They had so many skeletons there, so they decided to decorate the church with them."

"Cool!" I said and smiled. I knew I would search for more information about that place.

"And in Sagada, the Philippines, you can find coffins hanging off a cliff."

"They didn't bury them in the ground?"

"No. Many stories explain why they wanted to put them so high—for fear of their hunting enemies, or because they wished to be closer to the gods."

"Wow, this is so interesting!"

He told me more about some creepy legends he had heard about, and I laughed at his jokes.

While we were talking, I had this feeling this was the beginning of a great friendship.

This evening, I asked Mom whether we could invite Alex and Lily to our house again or do something together.

Mom was happy to see we both made friends.

"I told you so," she said with a smirk on her face, reminding me SHE IS ALWAYS RIGHT.

After I rolled my eyes at her, I admitted this whole island life was getting to be fun!

SATURDAY

Mom is very excited I made a friend.

Usually, moms are skeptical about letting their daughters hang out with boys, but not our MOM.

Mom believes that as long as boys are respectful to us girls and protective of us, they are better companions than girls who love drama.

So today, Mom and Dad invited Alex and Lily on our boat to take all of us snorkeling on the local coral reef.

I called Tracy to see whether she would like to join us, but her family had already made plans to visit relatives, so she couldn't come.

First, after a half-an-hour ride around the nearby islands, we stopped at an oceanfront park where we docked our boat.

The park is a popular tourist destination because of the azure waters and the broken bridge that used to be a railroad in the past.

We bought lunch and ice cream at the store there, and we enjoyed it at a picnic table overlooking the ocean.

Natalia and Lily wanted to play on the beach for a while, so we all took a walk on the sand.

While we were strolling, Alex whispered in my ear, "You know we are walking on poop, right?"

I looked at him, concerned he already had too much sun. "What do you mean we are walking on poop?"

"The parrotfish that live at the reef poop sand. The sand you are walking on right now," he said and smiled.

PARROTFISH, THE FISH THAT POOPS SAND

"Eww!" I said.

Everyone turned toward me.

"What happened?" Natalia asked.

"Alex said the sand is parrotfish poop," I said.

"Eww!" Natalia reacted. "Mom, is that true?"

Mom smiled. "Yes. Parrotfish feed on algae they scrape off dead coral that builds the reef. The undigested, ground-up coral becomes their poop and our sand."

"EWWWWW!!" all three of us girls reacted.

Alex laughed. "Told you! I'm full of useless information."

Dad smiled. "You will see many parrotfish at the reef this afternoon."

After that, Natalia and Lily decided NOT to play in the sand today, so we returned to the boat.

On the way to the reef, a pod of dolphins swam close by and hitched a ride on the waves we were making with our boat.

We were excited to see the dolphins jumping in and out of the water like we had created the best attraction ever!

Dad turned the boat and rode in large circles so the dolphins could stay with us, and it worked. They jumped through the waves happily.

"Remember that dolphins are not fish," Mom said.

Since we moved to the tropics, Mom takes every opportunity to give us an outdoor lesson about the islands and the marine life around us.

She continued, "They are mammals, just like all of us. They have lungs and breathe air through the blowhole. They can't breathe underwater. They need to come up for air, or they will drown."

"Dolphins can drown?" Natalia asked, surprised.

Mom nodded. "Yes. Just like us."

"What happens to a sick or an injured dolphin, then?" I asked.

"Other dolphins pick him up and carry him to the surface so he can breathe. We know of dolphins who rescued drowning people this way."

"Amazing," Natalia said.

Mom continued, "Do you know that each dolphin has a name, like a unique whistle he recognizes when other dolphins call him?"

"Is that why we often hear squeals near dolphins?" Lily asked.

"That's how they communicate with each other. But they also use echolocation underwater to catch fish they can't see in the dark."

"What's echolocation?" Natalia asked.

"When dolphins make clicking noises in the water, the sound bounces off objects near them, like fish hiding, and that's how they know where to find them."

We all looked at the jumping dolphins, excited they wanted to ride our waves.

Alex started making funny squeaks, imitating the dolphins.

Natalia, Lily, and I burst out laughing, but then we joined him, squealing as well.

When the dolphins swam away after a while, we headed for the reef.

We had fun jumping from the boat and swimming with the colorful fish that live on the reef.

We saw many parrotfish, and I think we all had a deeper appreciation for the fish after today.

Later, Natalia and Lily came back on the boat to eat some snacks, but Alex, my parents, and I continued to enjoy snorkeling.

However, I dove in deeper at some point, so the bottom piece of my swimsuit got loose, and the bikini part floated away in no time!

😮

Everyone had their snorkels on, so there was no place for me to hide.

I thought I was gonna die!

I screamed, but everyone thought I saw a shark, and instead of swimming AWAY from me, Mom, Dad, and Alex were right by my side!

I yelled for them to leave me alone and swim away from me immediately!

I had tears in my eyes.

Mom must have sensed something else was wrong and quickly shielded me from the boys' view.

She told them to return to the boat and asked Dad to throw us a towel.

Soon, I wrapped the towel around myself the best I could, considering I was still in the ocean.

The challenge was to get out of the water without everyone seeing me, but Mom told the boys to look away.

Mom always has a change of clothes, so I switched into my other swimming shorts.

When I noticed Alex's red cheeks, I burst out laughing because he looked even more embarrassed than I did, and I didn't think that was even possible.

After "the bikini incident," things felt quite awkward between Alex and me.

Every time he looked at me for the rest of the day, I felt my cheeks burning.

And when I glanced at him, the same thing was happening to his face.

So, now I am not rushing to see him anytime soon until we both erase that event from our memories!

SUNDAY

Now that my cast is off, it's time to focus on my middle school goal and earn some REAL cash.

Mom paid me extra money for removing dead palm fronds from her garden today, but I wish she just kept the money because I almost died!

First, let me tell you that walking through a garden in the tropics is like walking through a minefield.

Plants that survive in blazing sun, humidity, and salty air have the sharpest edges or spikes you can't even imagine.

When Mom told me to put on long pants and a shirt with long sleeves on a hot day, I thought she had too much sun already.

When she handed me gloves, a hat, and plastic protective glasses for my eyes, I seriously started doubting her sanity.

"I'm removing dead leaves, not fumigating the place," I said.

"If you go there with your bare skin exposed, you will look as if you had a fight with a cat," Mom said.

Great! So much to look forward to!

But as soon as I entered the garden, I was glad I was completely covered.

Every step I made, I brushed against bromeliads with razor-sharp edges.

I had to be careful not to get impaled by weird-looking Agave succulents that were as tall as me and had massive arms with sharp teeth and spines.

And when I tried to remove the dead fronds from pygmy palms, their spines were sticking out the side of my hand!

Then I understood the need for plastic glasses!

I also had to make sure I didn't touch any oleander plants because they are poisonous and deadly!

As a matter of fact, Mom told me most of the plants in the garden are poisonous if you eat them!

Plants like the oleander, the milkweed, and the periwinkle have colorful flowers and survive well near the ocean, but they are all toxic.

I wasn't planning to consume any of them, but I didn't want to touch them, either! Just in case!

Now, I don't know about you, but I don't need that type of stress in my life!

Every move I made put me in danger, and I had to inch my way through the garden.

You see, palm trees are very messy. They don't wait for the fall to drop their leaves. Their fronds turn brown and die all year long, which means dead leaves need to be removed every week.

And if you don't remove them, they will fall on your head when you least expect it.

And I'm not talking about tiny leaves. I'm talking about fronds that are larger than a person, and some weigh as much as me! So, trust me, you want them removed.

If palm trees are too tall, a professional company must trim them twice a year. They will also remove all the coconuts from coconut palms because nobody wants to be hit on the head with one of those!

Most of our palm trees are reachable, so it's up to us to remove the dead fronds. So, when I was trying to yank off some of the lighter leaves from the palm trees, I had to make sure I wouldn't get hurt around the sharp plants.

And if that wasn't enough, I also had to deal with small lizards that were inside every plant I touched, bopping their heads up and down.

The male lizards puff out their bright orange throat fans, called dewlaps, every time they see me.

They do it to intimidate me, but Mom says those tiny lizards are very useful in the yard because they eat pests like cockroaches.

Since cockroaches love heat, humidity, and living in the tropics, I decided to live in peace with the lizards.

Every time I managed to remove a dead palm frond that was larger than me, I needed to drag it to the driveway, bend it in half, and throw it into a trash can.

What a workout that was!

I seriously started doubting any amount of money was even worth such a job, but I kept going because Tracy complained I was doing nothing toward my goal.

"How are you gonna prove you are ready for middle school?" she asked the other day.

I was fine helping out in the yard, but I never imagined I would risk my life doing it!

When I was dragging one of the fronds, I almost stepped on a snake!

A SNAKE! IN OUR GARDEN!

The snake was as scared of me as I was of it, so we both rushed in opposite directions.

Trying to escape my imminent death, I tripped over a massive trunk and roots of this plant called a philodendron, and I ended up falling on some kind of animal!

It turned out to be an iguana, desperately trying to break free from underneath my body.

I don't know what it is with the iguanas and me, but they seem to be attracted to me like magnets.

Terrified the prehistoric-looking creature would bite me, I jumped away as quickly as I could.

The iguana hurried away, dropping and leaving its tail on the ground!

When I saw the tail was wriggling like a snake, as if it were still attached to the iguana's body, I collapsed and fainted.

When I gained consciousness, I was lying on a sofa in the living room with my whole family hovering above me.

Mom thought I had too much sun and had a heat stroke, so she was ready to take me to an emergency room right away.

The emergency room sounded good to me because I wasn't sure if I was in one piece or not.

Once you witness a disembodied wiggly tail, you can't ever erase this image from your memory.

When I inspected my body and saw no parts were missing, I finally told my family the truth about the snake and the iguana.

When I finished telling my story, Natalia screamed in terror. Surprisingly, Mom and Dad laughed.

"It's not funny," I said, insulted.

Mom said I had better get used to snakes and iguanas because they are common in the tropics.

"The snakes are not venomous, and they are beneficial in the garden because they feed on rats," Mom said. "And the iguana dropped her tail as a defense mechanism to escape freely from you. The iguana is fine, and it will grow another tail after a while."

Although Mom tried to make me feel better, I wasn't sure living in the islands was such a good idea anymore.

I don't think I have the guts to return to Mom's garden anytime soon, so whatever I've earned today will have to last me until I find other ways to get hold of some cash.

WEDNESDAY

Today, I was looking forward to my first workshop at the Art Club because making art is my favorite thing in the entire world.

I'm always doodling emojis in my notebooks because it's easier for me to communicate with art.

The art classes during school hours are great, but belonging to the Art Club is a different ballgame.

I was excited when Natalia and I joined it this week.

The art teacher divided all the kids into smaller groups. Natalia and Lily sat with kids their age.

I ended up at the table with Tracy, Alex, this girl whose name is Grace, and . . . BRITTANY!

I DON'T KNOW WHY LIFE ALWAYS HAS TO BE SO UNFAIR TO ME!!

All the boys drool around Brittany, so when we sat at our art table, it was only a matter of time before I expected Alex to forget I even existed.

But to my surprise, Alex didn't even notice Brittany.

He took a seat near me and asked me what I planned to create today.

Mrs. Picoli, the art teacher, said that we would be making pottery with wet, low-fire clay today, and I couldn't believe it!

I was so excited to work with clay for the first time!

Apart from drawings, I had never made anything I could use in real life!

As soon as I said I would make a bowl, all the girls at the table wanted to make bowls as well.

Only Alex decided to make something different—a vase.

Brittany grimaced. "I hope I won't destroy my brand-new dress doing this."

I didn't worry about creating a mess. But I worried about my ring. Dad gave it to me last year, and I promised I would never take it off.

So, I put the ring in front of me so it didn't get messed up with clay.

"That's a pretty ring," Brittany said. "Where did you get it? From the Pay-a-Penny store?"

Brittany's insulting comment hurt, but I decided not to reply because if there is one thing Mom always taught me, it is this:

NO RESPONSE IS BETTER THAN A WRONG ONE.

But Alex couldn't pass up the opportunity to stand up for me. "Brittany, your lousy comments are getting old!" he told her.

Brittany shrugged and pretended to focus on what the teacher was saying.

"I think your ring is very beautiful, Sylvia," Grace said and adjusted her glasses.

I smiled and thanked her. Grace is from Alex's class, and I already knew I would like her a lot.

Mrs. Picoli brought clay to our table and demonstrated how to shape it into different objects using our hands, special tools, and water.

We could create different objects by either pinching the clay into shapes we wanted or coiling, which means rolling the clay into snake-like rolls and layering them on top of one another.

We could also join rolled, flat slabs of clay to make things, but the teacher said it was a more challenging technique.

I decided to make a bowl for a dog because it's my dream to have a dog one day. I have been asking my parents to let me get a dog for years, but they still haven't bought one for me.

They keep telling me about all the responsibilities and commitments of having a dog at home, but I hardly ever listen.

One day, Mom will agree to get me one, and I will be ready when a cute little puppy enters our house.

I cut a flat piece of clay and pinched it into a mold that would give me the base of the bowl.

Then I rolled the extra clay into coils and attached a few rows of them to the top of my bowl.

For two pieces to adhere to each other, I needed to score, or scratch, them with a special tool and wet them with slip, which is a glue made with clay and water.

I decided to decorate my bowl with paws, so I pressed paw prints on the coils.

I glanced at my sister and noticed that Natalia shaped a funny-looking bowl by pinching the clay into an irregular shape, which looked great.

Grace's bowl looked like a little teacup, and she decorated it with flower stamps.

Brittany's bowl looked amazing—a smooth, perfectly round shape, decorated with little round seashell stamps.

She used the harder technique of working with a flat slab, which she rolled into a short cylinder and attached it to her bowl base.

Alex shaped his vase in a pretty cool way, but the weird-looking googly eyes sticking out of the vase were strange.

Tracy decorated her bowl with stamps of dresses and shoes—a true fashionista's masterpiece.

After two hours, we all finished, and the teacher collected our pottery.

The clay pieces need to dry for days, then the teacher will fire them in this special oven called a kiln, so when we come back in a week, we can paint them with glaze.

After we glaze them with colors, Mrs. Picoli will fire them again to make them waterproof and look polished.

Only after the third workshop will we take our pottery home.

When we all cleaned up our messes, I realized something was wrong.

MY RING WAS MISSING!!

I couldn't believe it!

My favorite ring was missing!

"My ring is gone!" I said. "Has anyone seen it?"

"Yes," Alex nodded, "it was on the table."

I looked at Tracy.

She shook her head. "I don't know where it is."

I turned toward Grace.

"I didn't take it. I swear!" she said.

I gave Brittany a stern look. She was the only one who had noticed the ring at all.

"Don't look at me that way. I didn't take your ring," she said, smiled, and walked away.

I felt tears welling up in the corners of my eyes, but no matter what, I knew I would not cry in front of all those kids.

I would cry at home, but not HERE.

Alex said he would help me look for it and told the teacher about my missing jewelry.

All the kids, except Brittany, started searching for my ring.

Brittany sat in a chair, browsing through Glamorous Teens magazine, waiting for the workshop to be over.

I didn't trust her—that's for sure!

Unfortunately, nobody found the ring, and when the class ended, many kids had to leave.

I felt really depressed about losing my favorite ring. How would I tell my dad?

The teacher promised me she would keep searching for it, and if she found it, she would call me right away.

I thanked Alex for helping me out and said goodbye.

I don't shed tears often, but I cried when I informed my dad about the missing ring.

Dad told me not to worry because he would eventually find me a different but similar one.

Still, his words didn't make me feel any better, and I sulked at home all night.

Nothing could cheer me up. Not my mom's apple pie, not even my sister's tries to make me laugh by making silly faces.

SATURDAY

It's been three days, and nobody has found my ring at the school's art studio. I checked with the art teacher on Friday, but so far . . . nothing.

Meanwhile, Natalia and I have been helping Mom around the house for the past few days.

We each cleaned our rooms and our bathroom, although neither of us dared to touch the toilet, so Mom had to do it.

I vacuumed the carpets while Natalia washed the floor.

We even helped with weeding in the garden until our knees were sore!

After doing chores around the house and outside, I was beginning to think that Mom was exploiting us for cheap labor.

But when Mom gave us thirty dollars as our new allowance, I decided it was worth it.

That kind of money could stack up pretty quickly, and I could achieve my goal in no time.

Natalia, of course, spent her money on another doll, which is a problem because she already has too many toys. They pile up in her room like crazy, and we can barely enter her room at this point.

Mom said it would be difficult for Natalia to clean a room with so many toys, and without cleaning it, there would be no allowance.

That just shows you that second graders are not ready to have their middle school goals figured out yet.

If I save my money for the future, I will be rich by the time I finish school and become an adult, and I won't have to work at all.

I ESTABLISHED MY MIDDLE SCHOOL GOAL!

When I called Tracy and told her I was making progress with my MIDDLE SCHOOL GOAL, she said her plan was not working out.

"Since my mom won't let me do makeup, and straightening my hair is out of the question, I decided to exercise and gain some muscles. . . . But I'm so sore, I can hardly move! Working out is HARD!"

"Why do you think I don't like sports?"

Tracy sighed. "How am I ever gonna look different?"

"You are asking the wrong person, girl. I know nothing about fashion."

"Maybe working out will help me do well during the relay races. What are you doing to prepare for them?" she asked.

"Nothing. I'm not planning to be there. I will fake some kind of illness and stay home," I said, proud of my plan. "Besides, who would choose me as her teammate?"

"I would," Tracy replied.

"Well, that would be a poor decision since we would lose miserably."

Tracy laughed, and we soon ended the call.

Me practicing for the races?

Yeah, right!

SUNDAY

This morning, I told Mom I had to study for my social studies test about Christopher Columbus's voyage to find a shorter road to Asia, which ended in "discovering" America.

I put discovering in quotes because we all know that Native Americans lived in the New World long before Columbus was born.

But I wish I hadn't told Mom about my test because as soon as she heard about it, she gave Natalia and me a lecture about Columbus's trip.

When she finished, Mom asked us what the names of the three ships of that expedition were.

I said, "The *Niña*, the *Pinta*, and the *Diarrhea*."

But Mom wasn't happy with my joke. "Sylvia!"

What? Considering what they were eating on those ships, I wasn't that much further from the truth.

Natalia raised her hand. "The *Niña*, the *Pinta*, and the *Santa Maria*."

Mom nodded and told us that many Europeans risked their lives to come to America.

The crossing of the Atlantic Ocean on the ships was hazardous, and the trips lasted weeks, even months, without seeing any land.

Then she told us we should watch the *Titanic* movie because it really showed the reality of such a treacherous trip.

"I want to watch *Titanic*, now!" Natalia said.

I sighed and turned toward my sister. "Let me spare you three hours of your life—they got on a boat, and the boat sank."

"Sylvia! Why would you spoil it for her?" Mom asked.

"I spoiled nothing. It happened for real, so I'm only educating her about history," I said with a smile.

"But I wanted to be surprised!" Natalia said.

We ended up watching the movie anyway. And I admit, I gained a deeper appreciation for all the people who leave everything and everybody behind to reach another country, searching for a better life.

When we finished watching the movie, Mom and Dad suggested we have a day trip to visit the replica of Christopher Columbus's ship displayed in the islands.

You see—this is the reason you should never tell your parents what you've been studying at school because they want to EDUCATE you even more.

And then parents wonder why kids don't want to talk about school!

We drove for about an hour before we reached the replica of *Santa Maria*.

When we entered the ship, I was surprised NOT to see any beds and learn that the crew members slept on the hard deck.

There were no bathrooms and no running water, so I could imagine how bad everyone smelled during the voyage.

At the bottom of the ship, in the hold, they kept their food in barrels, plus all kinds of trinkets they could trade with the natives.

We toured Columbus's tiny sleeping cabin with a desk where he wrote in his journal.

Unfortunately, today's inclement weather and the rough seas made the ship rock a lot, and soon I became seasick.

I told Mom I had to leave the ship or I would end up throwing up.

But she laughed and asked me if I could imagine traveling on a ship like this, searching for new lands for over TWO MONTHS.

I didn't think it was funny because, honestly, I couldn't imagine staying there for another MINUTE.

When we left the ship, Mom said that Christopher Columbus's plan to sail across the ocean to reach Asia was rejected many times by several important people.

Only after many years was he finally granted the ship to fulfill his dream.

But even during the voyage, his crew members tried to give up and sail back home.

Because of his determination and willpower, Columbus accomplished his goal.

He sailed across the Atlantic Ocean to find another place, although he never knew he reached new lands or how his expedition connected two worlds.

"So, I hope this shows you, girls, how important it is never to give up on your dreams, no matter how many obstacles stand in your way," Mom said.

Natalia and I listened to Mom, although I was already imagining reaching my goal of becoming filthy rich in the future.

One day, when I am very wealthy and won't know what to do with all my money, I will be happy I listened to Mom and never gave up saving my allowance.

MONDAY

I woke up in a bad mood today, and I carried on with sulkiness most of the afternoon.

I'm still upset that nobody has found my ring at the school's art studio. I really hoped someone would have found it by now!

On a positive note, I aced the test about Christopher Columbus's voyage, so I guess listening to Mom all Sunday long wasn't a total waste of time.

TUESDAY

"Did you see how Alex looked at you during PE today?" Tracy asked me during lunch.

"I don't know what you're talking about," I said.

But I knew EXACTLY what she was referring to. When we were outside on the field, every time I glanced at Alex, his eyes met mine, which sent goosebumps throughout my body.

"I caught him watching you several times!"

I smiled. "That's because we played on opposite teams. He probably was trying to figure out what my next move was."

Tracy made a skeptical face. "Yeah . . . right. Do you know what tomorrow is?"

"Not really."

"Valentine's Day! Are you going to give something to Alex?" she asked.

WHAT? TOMORROW?

"Um . . . I wasn't planning to. We're just friends," I said.

"Friends can give each other Valentine's Day cards."

"I don't think I would have the guts to hand him a card around all those kids in art class tomorrow."

But . . . Mrs. Picoli did say we would have a cupcake party for Valentine's Day, so maybe it would be okay to exchange cards with each other.

"Do you really think I should make a card for him?" I asked, hesitant.

"I think you should . . ." she said.

"Do we have to hand EVERYONE a Valentine's Day card, too?"

"Not at our school."

"Good."

I have given a hundred Valentine's Day cards to people over the years.

At many schools, they make you give one to everyone in the class, whether or not you like the person, which, to me, loses the real meaning of a Valentine's Day card.

But I had never given one to a boy I truly liked, someone I could be friends with forever.

"Maybe I will make one for Alex, then," I told Tracy.

Tonight, with a fluttering heart, I cut the colorful construction paper and folded it into a card.

I decorated it with smiley faces (I didn't dare to put any hearts!) and wrote inside:

Happy Valentine's
Day, Alex.
Thank You
For Being Such
A Great Friend!
Sylvia

I hope I will have the courage to give it to him tomorrow. . . .

WEDNESDAY

Today, Natalia and I woke up to the smell of freshly made pancakes.

When we joined our parents for the delicious breakfast, we were surprised to see boxes of chocolates and teddy bears waiting for us.

On the table stood a vase with red roses and a wrapped box for Mom.

"For my three special Valentines," Dad said and gave each of us a hug and a kiss.

We all thanked Dad and enjoyed a family breakfast together.

Later, during the workshop at the Art Club, I first searched for the ring again but couldn't find it.

I asked all the kids if anyone had seen my ring around or knew if someone had taken it, but nobody knew where it was.

I guess I'm not a skilled detective.

😔

I was still upset when we sat at the table with Tracy, Grace, Alex, and Brittany, although I told myself to let it go when the teacher brought our pottery.

It was pretty amazing to hold our creations in our hands.

The pieces were solid and white but still rough and not interesting.

Today, we were supposed to glaze them with colors so they could be fired into shiny objects.

Glazing pottery looks like regular painting. After firing in the kiln, the glaze coating will transform the pieces into beautiful, colorful, and waterproof ceramics.

Although I should have been excited to work on my art, I just couldn't get into it.

Then, Alex leaned toward me and whispered into my ear, "Can I speak to you in private?"

I said sure, and we walked into the hallway.

"I have something for you," he said and gave me a small box.

When I opened it, I couldn't believe my eyes!

THERE WAS A GORGEOUS SILVER RING INSIDE!!

"Happy Valentine's Day," Alex said.

I was speechless.

"I know it's not much . . ." Alex stuttered, "but I hope you would like to wear it . . . from me."

"Alex, it's beautiful!" I said.

His cheeks reddened. "It's a friendship ring."

"Friendship ring . . . I like it! Very much, actually! Thank you so much."

No boy had ever given me a ring before.

A million thoughts were running through my mind, questions of what I should do in a situation like this, and for once, I stopped overthinking it.

To say thank you, I kissed him on the cheek.

OMG! I KISSED A BOY!

I can't believe I had the guts to kiss a boy!

Like a friend, of course, but still!

"Um . . . I have something for you, too," I said, and I removed the handmade Valentine's Day card from the back pocket of my jeans.

It was wrinkled at the corners, but my pocket was the safest spot I could think of.

He opened the card and read it. "Did you make it yourself?"

I nodded. "Yes . . ."

"Thank you. I'll keep it forever," he said and looked deeply into my eyes.

We both quickly looked away and headed to our art table.

As soon as we sat down, Tracy's eyes opened wide in amusement.

"Did you get a new ring?" she asked.

I nodded.

Brittany, who had barely paid attention to me so far, also glanced at the ring.

"Alex," she asked, "did you buy the ring for Sylvia?"

He nodded.

Tracy and Grace immediately cried, "Aww!"

"How romantic," Brittany said with sarcasm in her voice.

While everyone was making a big deal out of my new ring, I wished they all would keep quiet.

This is why being around other kids is tough for me—
they behave like uncivilized creatures sometimes!

I paid no mind to them and focused on painting the
paws on my bowl.

But deep inside, I felt so happy!

After we painted our pottery, the teacher brought
heart-shaped cupcakes for everyone and paper art
supplies to make Valentine's Day cards for our parents.

After we enjoyed the delicious snacks, everyone got busy
decorating their cards.

Alex, Tracy, Grace, and I made extra cards to give to
Mrs. Picoli, and so did many other kids.

At the end of the class, Natalia received seven
Valentine's Day cards from the boys!!

I guess this kid steals more than just teachers' hearts!

I think the time has come for me to pay more attention to her strategy because it seems like she has it all figured out for sure!

On the way home, all Tracy could talk about was my ring from Alex.

"Wow! Sylvia, do you know what that means?" she asked.

I was kind of hoping she wouldn't read into it much and let it be, but it is Tracy, after all, and she dissects everything in her mind.

"No . . ."

"It means he likes you! Like, really likes you!"

"I hope he likes me because it would be hard to be friends if he didn't," I said and smiled.

Tracy sighed. "You know what I mean!"

I giggled.

I can't believe I already made two friends at the island school, and it wasn't as difficult as I had thought.

☺

FRIDAY

This morning, I was so excited because we had a field trip scheduled to the Marine Research Center, where we would interact with all kinds of animals that live in the ocean.

Both fifth-grade classes were going, so I knew Alex would be with us as well.

As soon as I arrived at school, the bus was waiting for everyone in the parking lot.

I took a seat near Tracy, and Alex sat with his friend a few rows behind.

Because of the friendship ring on my finger, I felt different . . . like I belonged to someone.

No longer THE NEW GIRL. No longer AN OUTSIDER.

Now I'm just THE ODD ONE.

But Mom always reminds me what Dr. Seuss said:

"YOU HAVE TO BE ODD TO BE NUMBER ONE."

And today, I felt like I was someone else's NUMBER ONE, no matter how odd I may seem to everyone.

Every time I glanced at Alex, he looked at me, and we both smiled.

As soon as we arrived at the center, we were directed to the sea lions.

When I touched their skin, I was surprised it wasn't smooth, the way it looked, but instead, it felt like fur.

We watched the trainers put medicine into the sea lions' eyes, and we listened to their lecture about those amazing creatures.

One trainer asked me to throw a ball to the sea lion in front of me, and when I did, the sea lion caught the ball on its nose and kept it there for a few seconds.

"Its whiskers help the sea lion hold the ball in place," said the trainer.

Later, we visited a lagoon with dolphins, where we learned about their habits, behavior, and silly antics.

Brittany wanted to be the first one to touch the dolphins, so she pushed through everyone standing near the dock, sending me over the edge.

IN MY CLOTHES AND BOOTS, I ended up flying into the water!!

My heart started beating like crazy because I knew our next stop was a lagoon with sharks, and I wasn't sure if they were connected or not.

What was worse, nobody even noticed I was in the water!

I guess I should have known nobody paid me any mind.

Everyone was mesmerized by the dolphins near the floating dock, where the trainers were busy lining up all the kids to meet them.

But then I heard a splash behind me, and I was surprised to see Alex swimming toward me, trying to catch his breath.

"Are you okay?" he asked.

I nodded.

"Follow me," he said.

Before I could say anything, two dolphins swam close to us as if waiting for a back rub.

I extended my hand flat on top of the water, and the dolphins rubbed against it.

I took care not to touch their blowholes through which they breathed.

"I think they want us to grab their fins . . ." Alex said. "I think they want to rescue us."

"Really?" I said and smiled.

When we gently grabbed the dolphins' fins, they took us for a ride around the lagoon.

I don't remember a day I had laughed louder than today when the dolphins pulled us behind them in a playful way.

Of course, everyone saw what was happening by now, and I could only imagine their surprised faces.

When the dolphins brought us to the floating dock near the spot where everyone was standing, the trainers frantically tried to pull us out of the water.

"How did you end up in the lagoon, kids?" one trainer asked.

"Sylvia fell into the water," Alex said, climbing onto the dock, "and I jumped in to help her out, but those two dolphins had it under control."

I didn't really want to leave the dolphins.

If it were up to me, I would spend a whole day swimming with those animals, but I knew the rest of the kids were dying to interact with them, too.

Of course, nobody would get into the water the way I did, so my encounter with the dolphins—as unexpected as it was—turned out to be the best experience ever.

Before I climbed onto the dock, I gave a kiss to "my" dolphin, who squealed with happiness.

It's funny how something that looked embarrassing— like me flying into the water with all my clothes— turned out to be one of the best things that happened to me today.

And who would have thought I had Brittany to thank for this fantastic day?

I was planning to thank her for "accidentally" pushing me into the lagoon, but when I saw her angry and jealous face, I let it go.

Oh well . . . I'm sure she had a chance to touch the dolphin for a second.

SATURDAY

This afternoon, when I was lounging by the pool, I received a text message from Alex.

A: Swimming with the dolphins with you yesterday was the best memory ever!

S: Yes! I couldn't believe how friendly and playful the dolphins were with us. . . . Thank you for jumping in to save me.

A: Anytime! I think I'm getting good at it by now.

S: That's because I'm ALWAYS in some kind of trouble!

A: You make my life interesting that way.

I felt my cheeks burning, so I was glad we were texting, and Alex couldn't see me blush.

S: Thank you for being such a good friend. Again . . .

A: Again . . . Anytime!

S: See you next week?

A: Can't wait!

WEDNESDAY

Today, when we entered the art classroom, all our ceramic pieces were proudly displayed on a table at the center of the room. They looked amazing!

They were shiny, strong, and sealed for us to use them with food and water!

All the kids congregated around the table to admire their art.

After a while, we grabbed our creations, amazed by our creativity.

"This is the cutest bowl for a dog I have ever seen," Grace said.

"Thank you," I replied.

"Do you have a dog?" she asked me.

"I wish! But one day, I know I will, and this is a bowl for my future puppy."

"That's great! I have a dog, so if you ever want to come over to my house, you can play with it."

"Really? That would be awesome!"

Grace told me she loves playing the BUILDING WORLDS game as much as I do, which is a total reason to get to know her better.

We exchanged our phone numbers and promised to set up a date to meet.

I looked around. Everyone was showing off their pottery.

With all the kids holding highly breakable ceramic items in their hands, it was only a matter of time before something destructive happened.

However, I never imagined I would be the cause of such mayhem.

But it wasn't entirely my fault!

I went to the restroom located in a dark hallway. The restroom was dark as well with just a dim light on.

When I was leaving, my eyes had a hard time adjusting to the bright light ahead, and something startled me as I entered the room where everyone was standing and talking.

Alex was holding his vase with the strange googly eyes, so it scared me for a second.

Staring at Alex's vase, I didn't notice someone's backpack on the floor, and I tripped over it, flying across the room.

Thank goodness I had put my bowl away before going to the restroom, but unfortunately, I crashed into Brittany, who dropped HER bowl on the floor.

The bowl shattered into tiny pieces, which sent Brittany into a fury!

And you will never believe what was lying near the broken pieces of Brittany's bowl!

My ring from my dad!

The ring was trapped in a dry piece of clay lying in the corner, and I recognized the seashell stamps on it right away!

Brittany must have rolled the clay over my ring, and the leftover piece of clay ended up on the floor! With my ring in it!

"Sorry I broke your bowl, but at least we found my ring!" I told Brittany and smiled.

By the look on her face, I was glad many kids in the room surrounded me. I wouldn't have wanted to be alone with her right then!

After everyone saw the ring in my possession, nobody paid any attention to Brittany fussing over her broken bowl.

I couldn't believe she wouldn't even apologize for trapping my ring in her clay!

That just shows you how selfish some kids are!

Before we left the workshop, Alex gave me another gift.

"You can't shower me with gifts like this," I said and laughed.

"I made it for you," he said.

I opened the gift bag, and you will never believe what was inside! The vase with four googly eyes!

LUCKY ME!

FRIDAY

The schoolwide relay races took place today, and as you know, I had been dreading this day for a long time.

I pretended to be sick this morning, hoping Mom would let me stay home. There was no way I would be embarrassing myself in front of my new friends!

But Mom didn't believe me one bit and said that she and Dad were going to the school to see the races, too.

ARE YOU KIDDING ME??

Now I couldn't do anything to get out of the competition!

All the other classes were canceled because this was an all-day event, so there was no other place I could possibly go.

Because I hadn't planned to be at school during the races, I didn't wash my usual PE outfit. So, guess what I was forced to wear today!

That's right—the sporty T-shirt and shorts Brittany gave me for my birthday!

OH, THE IRONY!

When we arrived at school, tons of parents were already waiting on the bleachers around the track.

Great! Not only was I going to embarrass myself in front of my friends and the entire school, but also in front of all those adults!

Kids were divided by grade on the field, so I wished Natalia good luck before she disappeared into her group.

As soon as I joined the fifth-grade group, Coach said he would choose eight leaders who would select their own teams of four runners.

Here we go, I thought.

I wished I had brought a good book to read because this would take a while. Since everyone knows I'm horrible at sports, I will be chosen last for sure.

"The team leaders have demonstrated strength and great teamwork throughout the year," Coach said. "For the fifth grade, please step up: Alex, Daniel, Michael, Thomas, Mark, Linda, Brittany, and Sabrina."

It did not surprise me to see the selection because those kids are really good at sports.

When Alex stepped up to announce his team, I knew he was close friends with some fast runners from his class, and he would choose the best team to win.

But to my surprise, the first name he called out loudly was . . . mine.

"Sylvia," Alex said.

I could swear my heart stopped beating when all eyes turned toward me.

"Me?" I asked, pointing to myself.

Alex smiled. "Yes, you."

I COULDN'T BELIEVE I WAS CHOSEN FIRST IN PE CLASS!

When I walked toward Alex and stood beside him, I said, "Are you crazy?"

He nodded. "Crazy for you."

My cheeks blushed, and my heartbeat accelerated.

Just splendid! I'm sure we will be the first ones! AT THE END, of course!

I sighed. "I hope you know I'm a turtle," I told him.

He looked at me and smiled. "You are not a turtle. You are turtle-y awesome."

I giggled. It takes Alex to make me laugh before the race!

Then Alex told me to choose another runner myself.

"Tracy! It's a no-brainer," I said.

When Tracy joined us, grinning from ear to ear, Alex told her to choose the last runner.

"Grace," she said.

And there we were, the four of us—Alex, Tracy, Grace, and me—a great group of friends and a team.

Unsurprisingly, Brittany chose her Squad, and the four girls cheered to be together.

The rest of the leaders chose their closest friends as well, so it looked like friendships won over running capabilities, but . . . maybe that's what teamwork is really about.

I don't know if you have ever seen relay races, but this is the drill.

The first runner runs around the track holding a stick called a baton. After he completes his run, he needs to hand the baton to runner number two so she can run the track with it, too.

When the second runner finishes her run, she passes the baton to runner number three, who will run the track until he reaches the fourth runner and hands over the baton.

The fourth and final runner runs around the track with the baton and finishes the race.

So . . . if one runner messes up, the entire team goes down.

NO PRESSURE AT ALL!!

After kindergartners and first graders ran first, I finally saw Natalia at the start of the track.

I recognized Lily on her team, so I was glad she had her best friend there.

But she didn't seem to be happy about it at all!

At first, I was confused. But when I realized who her other teammate was, I burst out laughing.

Of all the admirers and friends in her class, she was teamed up with MAX GUNOV!!

As I laughed, I couldn't help but notice she was fuming inside like a dragon about to release the fire from its mouth.

Seeing my sister going ballistic at the track was a highlight of my day!

All this anger must have put a fire up her bottom because when it was her time, Natalia ran the entire track in a flash.

And when Max took over, he finished the race with the speed of a rocket.

I think Natalia and Max didn't care about the rest of the contestants. They were competing with each other!

When I heard the names of the first-place winners for the second grade, my jaw hit the ground in shock.

Natalia and Max Gunov's team won!

I couldn't believe this kid outran everyone else in her grade!

And who would have known that she and Max Gunov could be such a great team, after all?

When the third graders lined up on the track, I became nervous and started sweating. I knew my time was coming.

I just couldn't stop thinking about how much I hated running. And what was worse, Alex, Tracy, and Grace were my teammates, so I was sure I would make them look bad!

The clock was ticking. . . . Our time was coming. . . .

When the fourth graders started their race, I took off, too. I ran away from my friends, from everyone, from this stupid race, and from guaranteed embarrassment.

I went to the opposite side of the school and sat down on the front steps. I couldn't stop the tears from rolling down my cheeks anymore.

Within a few minutes, I saw Alex, Tracy, and Grace running toward me.

"What are you doing? You need to get ready for the race," Alex said, trying to catch his breath.

I shook my head. "I can't do this! Why did you choose me? Why couldn't you choose someone who actually loves running? I don't want to embarrass myself!" I said, crying.

"You will be fine—" Alex said before Tracy interrupted him.

"Embarrass yourself?" Tracy added with anger. "Don't you think it's too late for that? We are your team, and we count on you. But you can only think about yourself right now!"

Grace put her hands on her hips. "We are not only a team. We are your friends. Doesn't that mean anything to you?"

I looked at the ground and sighed. "It means everything to me."

Alex sat down next to me. "I chose you because I knew you could do well in sports if you REALLY tried. And I wanted you to run with your friends instead of some kids you barely know."

I looked at him, wiping away the tears with my hand. "But if you chose a team with fast runners, you would have a chance of winning."

"Excuse me!" Tracy said. "We are standing right here!"

"Exactly! Who said we are slow runners?" Grace asked.

I burst out laughing, and so did everyone else, too.

Alex put his arm around my shoulders. "It doesn't matter if we win, as long as we give it our best and do it TOGETHER as friends."

"And you all won't be mad at me if I trip and we lose because of me?" I asked.

"No," Tracy said. "Whether or not you like it, you're a part of this pack now, and we need to stick together."

It felt so good to be liked and needed. It felt wonderful to finally have friends who really cared about me.

I nodded and stood up. "Okay then. Let's go!"

"And you were wrong on the first day of school, Sylvia," Tracy said as we walked toward the track. "There are many interesting things about you."

I smiled and gave her a hug. "Thank you."

Alex grabbed my hand and directed me toward the track to join the other fifth-grade runners.

"Let's do it!" Alex said and told me to position myself at my start line.

Alex chose our positions on the track. Grace was supposed to run first because she was fast. Tracy would be second. Then me. Alex would finish the race.

As soon as the race started and Grace ran around the track, I was pleased to see that some other teams were slow, so maybe I wouldn't be the only disaster around here.

The girl from Brittany's Squad came in first, but Grace was second, so we had a pretty good start when it was Tracy's turn to run.

She maintained the second spot with ease, and I was impressed with her running capabilities.

When Tracy reached my spot, I grabbed the baton from her hand and ran as quickly as I could.

Because my team counted on me, I forgot about the entire world around me and focused on the race.

I ran and ran until I reached Alex at his start line.

I handed the baton to him, and he took off like the roadrunner from cartoons I used to watch as a little kid.

It was him against the fastest runners, which meant Brittany was the fourth runner, too.

The only problem was . . . I left Alex with a fourth spot, and Brittany was already in first.

I wasn't sure whether I should wish that Brittany would fall down in the middle of the race. So, I did what came naturally to me—I wished that Brittany would trip.

But . . . unfortunately, she didn't. In fact, she was super fast, and that's when I realized I just couldn't measure up to her. Brittany and her Squad finished their race as fast as lightning.

The fastest runners were so close to one another that I couldn't tell who came in first, second, or third.

We had to wait for Coach's verdict.

As soon as all the grades were done with the races, Coach positioned three podiums in the center of the track. Then, he took out medals and announced the winners from each grade.

Natalia's team stood proudly on the highest podium, and even Max Gunov, standing beside her, didn't erase the grin on her face.

When it was time for the fifth grade, it did not surprise me to hear that Brittany and her Squad won first place. Of course they did!

When they stepped on the highest podium, I wished I had been up there. But that's just a silly dream because I'm so slow!

Daniel's team was second. As they received their medals, I felt a pang of jealousy filling my heart.

Then, something unexpected happened.

I heard my name.

"Alex, Sylvia, Tracy, and Grace—our third-place winners," Coach said.

WHAT??

How could that be possible?

And yet, there we were—stepping onto the third podium, receiving our medals.

"Good job, partner," Alex murmured in my ear.

I smiled. "Sorry I slowed you down. Without me, I'm sure you would have won first place," I told him.

"I prefer third place with you over first place with someone else," Alex said, looking into my eyes.

My heart melted when he said it, and the joy of winning consumed me when Coach placed a medal around my neck.

I had never received a medal for doing sports! Or doing anything else, for that matter!

"Sylvia, we are so proud of you!" Grace said.

"You did good," Tracy added and gave me a hug.

"Great teamwork," Coach said to all of us.

I smiled and looked around. Mom and Dad were standing and clapping, and all the parents cheered for the winners.

And then something unimaginable happened.

Brittany came over to me and said, "Third place... Not bad. Congratulations to you and your team."

When she extended her hand, I shook it. "Thanks," I said, stunned to see her being friendly with me for the very first time. "Your outfit must have brought me luck.

And congratulations on winning the fifth-grade race."

"Thank you. We should all celebrate at the ice cream place near the school," Brittany said and walked away.

Later that evening, Alex, Tracy, Grace, and I enjoyed our ice cream at a table with Brittany and her Squad, plus Daniel and his team. Natalia and her friends sat nearby, talking and laughing.

As if we had been friends forever.

As if nothing else mattered in the world.

SATURDAY
Today, I couldn't focus on doing the chores around the house. All I did was stare at my beautiful new ring.

It's one thing to get jewelry from your family; it's an entirely different thing when you receive it from a boy.

Can you behave silly when you have a ring from a boy on your finger?

I don't think so . . .

It seems embarrassing to allow such childish behavior.

One may even agree that the time has come to grow up at this point. Don't you think?

And this brings me to my MIDDLE SCHOOL GOAL.

Maybe saving my money for my future self to hire a staff to wait on me hand and foot is a slight exaggeration?

I mean . . . I can always worry about it later, right?

I think I should do something better with my allowance.

Something admirable.

Something helpful.

Something MIDDLE SCHOOL WORTHY!!

And I think I may have just the right idea . . .

MY NEW MIDDLE SCHOOL GOAL!

SUNDAY

Today, we had Tracy, Grace, Alex, and Lily come over to our house.

Dad served us homemade lasagna at the dining room table, and Mom baked a cake, which was a surprise because she rarely bakes desserts.

Tracy surprised everyone with her brand-new look—she had her hair cut shorter and dyed lighter brown!

"You look so different! Good different!" I told her as soon as I saw her.

"Thanks. I feel like I'm finally ready for middle school," she said.

While we sat at the table with my whole family, Mom and Dad complimented Tracy on her new appearance, although I knew they would never allow me to dye my hair.

"I will be honest with you," Tracy said to everyone. "I wish I hadn't done it."

"Why?" I asked.

"Yesterday, I really wanted to lighten my hair, so I dyed it myself. But I must have done something wrong because my hair turned carrot orange!"

"No!" I said, and we all started laughing.

"It wasn't one of those beautiful and unique orange colors people have naturally. . . . I looked like a carrot, and I cried all night!"

We couldn't stop laughing.

"So, this morning, my mom had to take me to a salon, and they fixed it with this light brown color. I had my hair cut shorter because my mom said all that dyeing destroyed the ends of my hair."

I almost fell from my chair, laughing.

"So, I'm not planning to dye my hair for a very long time!" Tracy added. "Or try to change my looks . . ."

"I think you are perfect just the way you are," I said.

When we stopped laughing, Tracy asked me how my MIDDLE SCHOOL GOAL was going.

"Did you earn money for your future plan?" she asked.

"What future plan?" Mom asked.

"Sylvia plans to save money to hire—"

"I did earn some money doing chores around the house and on the property," I interrupted, "but I decided to spend my first savings on something else."

Everyone looked at me with curiosity.

"I would like to donate it to the Marine Research Center . . . and maybe ask them if I could volunteer to help with the animals there in my free time."

I had been thinking about it for the past few days. Like my inner voice was telling me that was my true MIDDLE SCHOOL GOAL, after all.

Everyone looked at me, surprised.

"That's so cool," Alex said.

"Honey, that's wonderful! Such a grown-up thing to do!" Mom said and smiled.

"I actually do feel more grown up . . . and different. Like I'm kind of ready for middle school now," I said.

Mom smiled. "You mean no more chasing games in Grandma's barn and climbing through windows?"

Everyone laughed.

"Very funny!" I said, then I burst out laughing, too.

Later, Tracy said to me, "Your MIDDLE SCHOOL GOAL is totally better than mine!"

:)

I smiled.

After our meal, we all jumped into the pool and played water games until dark.

When we played pool volleyball, I teamed up with Mom, my sister, and Tracy against Dad, Alex, Lily, and Grace.

I thought my sister would slow us down, but I forgot how competitive she was, so I was glad she was on my team.

Natalia and I passed the ball to each other so the one closer to the net could throw it over to the opposite side.

We all laughed like crazy, splashing each other in the meantime.

When we won, I was so proud of my little sister. After all, we made quite a team!

Later, I climbed into her bed and said, "I'm happy we moved to the tropics and went to the island school. And I'm glad to have a sister like you."

She hugged me and asked, "Best friends forever?"

"Of course!" I said and smiled.

It was a perfect day!

☺

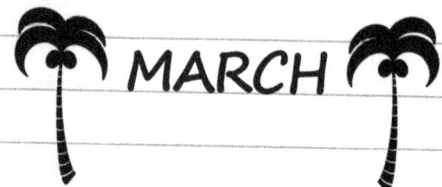

MARCH

MONDAY

Okay, I will admit that living on an island turned out to be a lot of fun!

Mom and Dad started taking us fishing on our boat on the weekends.

The only problem is that neither Natalia nor I like to kill the fish. So, every time we catch something, Dad needs to release it back into the water. Which doesn't make him very happy. . . .

I have little luck catching fish, but it probably has something to do with the fact that I daydream instead of watching my rod.

Occasionally, Dad catches some big fish.

But the funniest part is that my sister is actually better at fishing than my dad.

Although he taught her a lot, she took it to the next level and watched online videos about the sport.

She knows fancy words for all kinds of things, like a jig, a lure, chumming, or a strike.

She hooks the slimy squid on her own, while I never even touch it!

YUCK!!

And believe it or not, she catches more fish than Dad!

Because we live near a coral reef, we snorkel all the time.

Mom loves teaching us marine biology, and she often explores the reef with us. She wants us to know EVERYTHING about the ocean and the animals that live in it.

My favorite thing is to interact with dolphins who live nearby!

HOW COOL IS THAT?!

Who would have thought I would have so much fun living on an island!

I can tell spring has just begun.

SATURDAY

I wish I could tell you about wildflowers and butterflies dancing in the air, or something similar like that which SCREAMS spring has sprung, but that would be just too normal.

I know spring is here because I can hardly breathe! And it has nothing to do with anxiety this time!

But no matter how much the seasonal allergies bother me, I am excited because of several completely different reasons:

1. I have made some great friends on the island, like Alex, Tracy, and Grace, so I'm looking forward to our spring field trips and weekend hangouts.

I can already imagine us hitting the beach or lounging at the pool somewhere, sipping on frozen smoothies with a slice of orange and those cute little umbrellas.

2. I have donated my savings to the Marine Research Center, and they will allow me to help them with the dolphins and the sea lions!

3. I am on my way to middle school, which means I can't be considered a kid anymore!

MIDDLE SCHOOL, HERE I COME!

WHAT COULD POSSIBLY GO WRONG, RIGHT?

THE END

Dear Reader,

If you enjoyed reading this diary as much as I loved writing it, please leave a review on Amazon, Goodreads, or any online retailer of your choice. It's not easy to share your deepest secrets with someone you don't know, so I would be happy to hear from you. I'm curious what you think about my diary, and I will read every review for sure! Please ask an adult to help you.

Thank you!

Sylvia White

Artist: Sylvia White

DON'T MISS

MISHAPS IN PARADISE: THE PANDEMIC.
BOOK 2

ORDER ONLINE OR AT YOUR LOCAL BOOKSTORE.

WHAT COULD POSSIBLY GO WRONG?

How many times have I promised myself I would never ask this **STUPID QUESTION!!**

Because every time I do, something **COMPLETELY UNIMAGINABLE HAPPENS!**

You heard me right! As my life has proven many times before: **EVERYTHING CAN GO WRONG!!**

This is just my luck!! When I finally met cool people,

I'M NOT ALLOWED TO SEE ANYONE!

Now, when I'm itching to go outside to hang out with my new friends, they want me to stay home!!

ARE YOU KIDDING ME?

Now that I can't go anywhere, I want to go **EVERYWHERE!!**

I'm dying here!! I will even do PE! Just get me out of my house!!

Do you want to know what happened?

THE PANDEMIC HAPPENED!!

FROM THE AUTHOR

Since I was fifteen years old, I have traveled to various tropical places in the world, but my dream to live in the islands finally came true when I moved to the Florida Keys in 2014, a place I will always call home.

Many ideas for this book came from events that happened in real life. When I was a kid, I loved playing pranks on my family. I used to climb through windows, scraping my knees and breaking flowerpots.

I didn't want to grow up at all until one day, in fifth grade, a boy gave me a ring. At that moment, something changed. Sound familiar?

When I was in fifth grade, I competed in relay races with a baton, and my team won first place. After that victory, I started believing in myself and realized I was good at sports.

In middle school, I wanted to look different and more mature. I asked my mom if I could dye my blond hair brown, but she refused. I didn't listen, though, and I did it anyway. The color turned out to be a disaster, and I looked awful! To teach me a lesson, my mom made me keep the color for one year until my natural hair grew back, and we cut the dyed ends off.

Even back then, I wrote stories, dreaming of becoming a published author.

Although the Mishaps in Paradise diaries are fictional stories, they are inspired by my childhood and my two daughters, Olivia and Claudia, who are also three years apart and very different.

Olivia is a lot like Sylvia—reserved and shy around other kids. She doesn't enjoy doing sports, likes scary stories, and loves wearing boots.

Claudia is three years younger than Olivia, and she is the social butterfly in our family. She easily finds friends everywhere she goes (Olivia is rolling her eyes).

The story about Cinco de Mayo is true, and the girls share a birthday weekend!

My daughters often look for ways to earn money. When they were younger, they loved sneaking out on the street with a wagon full of things they were trying to sell to our neighbors.

Claudia loves fishing with her dad, and she even puts the slimy squid on the hook by herself!

Yuck!

Living on an island can be fun. We love snorkeling near the local coral reef, where we see many dolphins and parrotfish!

On our islands, we encounter plenty of chickens, iguanas, lizards, snakes, and alligators. And yes, on the rare days when the temperature drops to mid-40s F in South Florida, usually in January, frozen iguanas fall from the trees.

Here, we visited the replica of Santa Maria, the ship on which Columbus reached the New World.

For years, the girls attended art classes at the local art studio and made beautiful pottery.

I wish this were a fictional story, but here it is—Olivia with a broken wrist in a cast.

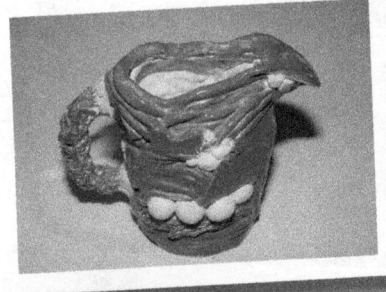

And this is the famous vase with googly eyes, made by the girls' Uncle Johnny when he was a teenager. I know he would be happy to see that it made it into the book.

Thank you for reading the Mishaps in Paradise diaries, and I hope you will enjoy the rest of the series! — Eva Polizze

ACKNOWLEDGMENTS

My publishing journey would have never started without a team of hardworking people who made this dream a reality.

First, I want to thank my daughters, Olivia and Claudia, for their dedication and support for this project. The days we spent working together I will cherish forever!

I could not complete these books without the help of my husband, Anthony, who had to hold down the fort when I spent long hours writing. I thank you with love.

I want to thank my mom, who sent me to Spain when I was fifteen so I could see the world. You ignited my love for the tropics, and look where it got me! I live on an island now! I'm sorry that I broke flowerpots, climbing through windows, that I didn't listen and dyed my hair anyway, and for all the other shenanigans.

I am forever grateful to my editor, Jennifer Rees, for her invaluable advice on making these series the best they can be and for loving Sylvia and Natalia as much as I do! It means a lot to me!

Many thanks to Emily Fritz for her patience in designing this book with me. I appreciate your hard work and commitment to this project, and I look forward to working with you on the next book in the series!

To Kateryna Korolova for the beautiful illustrations of the characters. They look stunning!

To Goran Tovilovic for designing the most beautiful cover Sylvia and Natalia could ask for!

To my proofreader, Tiffany Perry, for making sure we deliver the best version of the book to the kids.

To my legal team at Johnson & Dalal—Jade Taylor, Pascal Peng, and Mark Johnson, Esq. for your legal advice and work on the Mishaps in Paradise trademark.

To Matthew P. Molle for your assistance throughout the years.

And last, but certainly not least, to all the readers who enjoy the Mishaps in Paradise books. I hope I made you laugh.

ABOUT THE AUTHOR

Eva Polizze has been drawn to islands since she was a little kid. When she was fifteen, she attended a summer camp in Spain, where she fell in love with palm trees and warm climate regions for life.

When she was seventeen, she won first place in a national writing competition and was awarded a trip to Italy and a three-week vacation in Corsica. After that, she knew she would always be a writer and an island girl.

Over the years, she has traveled to many tropical places in the world, but her dream to live in the islands finally came true when she moved to the Florida Keys in 2014, a place she will always call home. Living on a small tropical island, surrounded by turquoise waters, jumping dolphins, and friendly Key deer, she writes about the island life in her books.

Eva Polizze is the author of the Mishaps in Paradise diaries, a middle school series about two sisters experiencing humorous misadventures on a tropical island. She has two daughters, Olivia and Claudia, who are her inspiration for the books.

You can visit her website at www.evapolizze.com

Find Eva Polizze on:

Printed in the USA
CPSIA information can be obtained
at www.ICGtesting.com
LVHW042054261023
762248LV00003B/37

LIAM AND THE GIANT EELS

ANN MALASPINA

An imprint of Enslow Publishing

WEST **44** BOOKS™

Please visit our website, www.west44books.com.
For a free color catalog of all our high-quality books,
call toll free 1-800-398-2504.

Cataloging-in-Publication Data

Names: Malaspina, Ann, 1957-
Title: Liam and the giant eels / Ann Malaspina.
Description: Buffalo, NY : West 44, 2025. | Series: West 44 MG verse
Identifiers: ISBN 9781978597549 (pbk.) | ISBN 9781978597532 (library
bound) | ISBN 9781978597556. (ebook)
Subjects: LCSH: Family--Juvenile fiction. | Friendship--Juvenile fiction. |
Hurricanes--Juvenile fiction. | Eels--Juvenile fiction. | Kayaking--Juvenile
fiction.
Classification: LCC PZ7.1.M289 Li 2025 | DDC [F]--dc23

First Edition

Published in 2025 by
Enslow Publishing
2544 Clinton Street
Buffalo, NY 14224

Editor: Caitie McAneney
Designer: Tanya Dellaccio Keeney

Photo Credits: Cover (background) smartboy10/iStock.com.

Printed in the United States of America

CPSIA compliance information: Batch #CS25W44: For further information contact
Enslow Publishing LLC at 1-800-398-2504.

Find us on

*For my parents, who've always
followed their consciences.*

PART 1

THE GREEN CHAIR

The green chair
    on the deck
        stood empty.

    No one touched it.
    No one sat in it.

They pretended it wasn't there.

Just like the stuff
    in Gramps's bedroom.

One evening in July,
    a bird
        landed
           in the chair.

"Could it be an osprey?" Liam asked.

Gramps loved watching the ospreys
    fly along Blackwater Creek.

"It's only a gull," Mom said.

One of a million scavengers
    begging for scraps
    at the Jersey Shore.

Bummer.

EARLY MORNING

at Sandy Cove Beach,

  Pink bubblegum sky.

  Joggers (including Mom)
    on the boardwalk.

  Matt the lifeguard, half-asleep.

  Umbrellas opened
    on the white sand.

And a flat, green, boring ocean.

WAITING

Liam floated
on his boogie board.

Waiting for
          something—
anything—
          to happen.

What a loser of a summer.

No waves.
No friends.
No blue crabs in his crab pot.
No Gramps.

A Jet Ski shot past Liam.

His board flipped
like a pancake.

"Way to go, Liam!"

Matt the lifeguard
put up his thumb.

ROSIE

"Hey, folks! Got any paintings for me?"

> A woman in a huge blue dress
> was setting up the Art Tent
> on the boardwalk.

Gramps's old friend, Rosie.

> Coco, the parrot,
> sat on her shoulder.
> He was eating a grape.

Mom shook her head. "Sorry, Rosie, not today."

> Liam had noticed Mom
> wasn't painting much this summer.

Rosie peered at him.

"Seen anything odd, young Liam?"

TIMES LIKE THIS

Rosie leaned on her cane.
"What about the crabs?"

How did Rosie know about the crabs?

Liam's crab pot
had been empty for weeks.

"Something odd is going on."
Rosie shook her head.

"Times like this,
I wish your gramps were here."

And now she was reading Liam's mind!

Lifting his wings, Coco squawked.
"Keep your eyes peeled!"

GRAMPS

At least Rosie
talked about Gramps.

Mom never wanted to.
She never even said his name.

Liam didn't, either.
It hurt too much.

But if you never say
a person's name,

you may forget about them.

SURPRISE

Liam braked his bike
at Gramps's seashell driveway.

He reached
into the mailbox
like he did every day.

Something—

      warm,
           slimy,
                 alive

(and definitely not mail)—

jumped out
like a birthday surprise.

Only Liam's
12th birthday
was a month ago.

"Whaaat!"

SLIDE, SLITHER, SLIP

The animal climbed up
Liam's right arm.

It crawled across his shoulders.

Slid to the ground.
Slithered across the driveway.
Slipped across the road.

Liam watched in shock
as it
DISAPPEARED
into the storm gutter.

Was this the
"something odd"
Rosie was talking about?

NOT A GARTER SNAKE

"Probably a harmless garter snake."
Mom was grilling turkey burgers
on the back deck.

"What about this?" Liam asked.
He showed Mom the only mail today.

A postcard from Liam's Aunt Cissy.
The top of the Eiffel Tower was chewed off!
"Wish you were her—"
was all they could read.

Liam had never heard of
a garter snake that ate postcards.

"Strange," Mom said.

THE SALT MARSH

Liam looked out
    at the scene he knew by heart.

The grassy yard sloping down
    to Gramps's dock.

Gramps's dock dropping off
    into Blackwater Creek.

Blackwater Creek zigzagging
    through the salt marshes.

The salt marshes stretching
    to the Atlantic Ocean.

Every summer, Liam and Mom
    stayed at Gramps's cottage on the creek.

Mom worked on her paintings.
    Liam fished with Gramps and boogie boarded.

He watched a pair of swans glide up the creek.
    Dragonflies swooped in the air.

The marsh looked the same as always,
    but it felt different to Liam.

And it wasn't just that Gramps was gone.

KAYAK

Before Liam could think any more,

> splashing paddles
>> broke the silence.

A red kayak raced down Blackwater Creek.

> It was heading
> straight
> for
> Gramps's
> dock.

CRASH!

The girl paddling the kayak
fell into the water.

"I can't swim! Save me!"

From the deck, Mom yelled,
"Then stand up,
for goodness' sake!
It's only two feet deep!"

Standing still,
the girl stared at the water.

The creek was dark as tea
from the iron in the sand.

"Have you seen any?"

She was tall like Liam.
Her black hair tied in two braids.

Liam knew exactly
what she meant.

"Yep," he called back.
"In the mailbox."

TRASH CANS

"They're eels, but huge!"

The girl spread her arms.

They were everywhere!

"My dad saw one at the Wawa.
Eating Swiss cheese.
Our neighbor found one in her trash can."

Liam gulped. Putting out the trash was his job.

"They don't look normal!"

What's a normal eel?
Don't all eels look weird?

That's when Liam saw

the thick bandage
on her right ear.

Now, that wasn't normal!

CIELA LIKE THE SKY

Liam ran to the dock
to help her out of the water.

"I lost my paddle."

High tide was pushing upstream.

The girl's paddle was probably
gone for good.

"What's your name?" Liam asked.

"Ciela," she said, pointing up.
She said it like SEE-ella.
Then explained:
"Same as the sky. In Spanish."

Mom called down.
"Why don't you join us
for lunch, Ciela?"

ZOMBIE

"A zombie bit it,"
Ciela mumbled, munching her burger.

She must have seen Liam
staring at her ear.

"You're joking, right?"

Did she really believe in the walking dead?

Besides, if a zombie bit her ear,
wouldn't she be . . .?

Liam changed the subject.
"Do you have a boogie board?"

"I can't swim, remember?"

She offered her two-person kayak.

"We can look for giant eels."

Liam grabbed a life jacket,
two paddles,
and two fishing hats
from the garage.

"Let's go."

RULES OF THE CREEK

Life jackets
and a one-hour
time limit

for being out
on Blackwater Creek.

On foot along the shore,
or on the water.

Mom's rules of the creek.

And Liam had to carry
his cell phone.

Turned on.

He hadn't broken
her rules, yet.

EGRET, TURTLE, BASS

The kayak moved fast down the creek.
In the back seat, Ciela was an ace paddler.
Much stronger than Liam.

But, every few minutes, she slowed down.
"What's that?"

And Liam told her:

A snowy egret standing like a statue.

A diamondback terrapin bobbing in the creek.

A striped bass racing downstream.

Gramps was the one who knew the marsh.
Liam just listened.

"What's that?"

A bird with a long beak pecked at a shell.

"I don't know its name."

Sometimes, Liam wished he'd listened harder.

BUGS

The marsh was also full of bugs.

"Get away!" yelled Ciela,
swatting the air.

Lots of bugs.

Mosquitoes, gnats,
horseflies,
and greenheads.

You never forget a greenhead bite.

"Part of the ecosystem,"
Gramps always said.
"And food for the dragonflies."

But something else was
1,000 times worse
than a greenhead,
according to Gramps.

A huge blue dome rose in the distance.
The Blackwater Creek Power Plant.
The oldest nuclear power plant in the country.

"See any eels?" Liam shouted to Ciela.

"Nope, not yet."

CRAB POT

The next morning,
Liam lay on the dock
and tugged
on the wet rope.

The crab pot,
a metal cage with
a trapdoor,
rose to the surface.

Empty, again.

(Except for a snail, marsh grass,
and a rusty bottle cap.)

Liam had only caught
      one blue crab all summer.

"I wonder why," Ciela said.

GONE

Ever since Liam was little,
Gramps let him have
his own crab pot.

Liam dropped fish
heads in the pot
every night.

He pulled up the pot
and took out the crabs
every morning.

Blue crabs and boiled corn
was a favorite meal for
him and Gramps.

Now Gramps was
gone. So were
the crabs.

LOBSTER TANK

Liam saw his second giant eel
at the Stop and Go Market.

Swimming in the lobster tank
with all the lobsters!

A little boy yelped.
Shopping carts crashed.
Apples and eggs went flying.

The giant eel slid from the tank.
Slithered onto the floor
and slipped out the back door.

"What the heck was that?"
"Did you see its teeth?!"
"Where did it go?"

YIKES.

NO DONUTS

Ciela was waiting outside with the bikes.

"Where are the donuts?"

Liam had lost his voice.

"Are you okay?'

He shook his head.

"Eel?"

"Yeah . . ."

"In the market?"

"Yeah . . ."

"Yikes."

"Mr. Burr. We gotta go see him."

"Who's Mr. Burr—and what about the donuts?"

"You'll see—and we'll stop at the Wawa."

THREE OLD FRIENDS

Always the three of them.
    Gramps, Rosie, and Mr. Burr.

    Fishing on Blackwater Creek.
Bird-watching in the marsh.
    Walking on the boardwalk.

(Their walks were mostly
    sitting on a bench
        and talking.)

The three old friends
    did something else, too.

INVESTIGATING

Gramps called it
        INVESTIGATING.

**Why don't more people in Sandy Cove
        recycle bottles and cans?**

**Who's using the rat poison
        killing the songbirds?**

**Why did the village
        chop down the white oak tree?**

The three old folks didn't
        always get answers.

But they never stopped
        asking questions.

BEACH ROAD

Liam and Ciela pedaled easily
      up Beach Road.
The wind was on their backs.

Sandy Cove lay at sea level.
      Without big hills, biking was easy.
But summer storms could hit hard.

Flooding was worse every year.
      Last year's hurricane
turned Beach Road into a river.

"How far are we going?" yelled Ciela.
      Liam leaned his bike around a curve.
"We're almost there."

SCARECROW

They rode past Ivan's Peach Orchard
and Bernie's Bait Shack.

"There it is!" shouted Liam.
A white house stood back from the road.

Paint peeling.
Squirrels on the roof.
Sweet corn in the yard.

A scarecrow waved at
Ciela and Liam.

"Strange!" whispered Ciela.

She rode up
the driveway
anyway.

MR. BURR

An old man sat on the porch in a rocking chair.

He had a long, white beard
and a cat on his lap.

"It's me—Liam!"

Mr. Burr hadn't seen his own hands
in over 50 years.

But he looked straight
at Liam and Ciela.

"I was wondering
when you two would show up."

BUZZING BEE

Mr. Burr stroked the cat's orange fur.

He listened
      to Liam tell about
            the giant eel in the mailbox—
      and Ciela tell about
            giant eels everywhere else.

Then he looked up at the sky.

You could hear . . .

      The cat purring.

      A bee buzzing.

      Ciela's sneaker tapping.

In the quiet, Liam might have heard time passing.

QUIET

Liam was used to quiet.

Gramps fell quiet whenever Liam
shared a problem.

First his grandfather would listen to him.

Then Gramps would think about what
Liam said.

At last, in his grumbly voice,
Gramps would give his honest opinion.

GRAMPS'S JOURNAL

Mr. Burr cleared his throat.
"Have you read your Gramps's journal?"

What journal?

Gramps never sat still.
He didn't have time for a journal!

The cat jumped off Mr. Burr's lap.
She hissed in Ciela's face.

"I'm out of here!" Ciela shouted. "Your cat is scary!"

The bandage was still on her ear.
Was she sort of acting like a zombie?

"You'd best read it!" Mr. Burr called after them.
"Then you might want to . . . investigate."

FOG

A thick fog moved in overnight.

Gramps's dock, Blackwater Creek,
and the salt marsh
disappeared.

Was this how the world
looked to Mr. Burr?

Yet, somehow,
Mr. Burr saw things
more clearly
than most people.

BIG DEAL

"Journals are private," Liam said.

Ciela rolled her eyes.

"You're just scared
          to go into your grandfather's room."

"No, I'm not."

Actually, he was.

Poking into Gramps's stuff
          would be like scratching
                    a mosquito bite—

Scratching makes the itch worse.

"What's the big deal?"

LOW TIDE IN THE SALT MARSH

"What are you painting?"
Liam asked, later.

Mom wasn't actually painting.
She was staring at the canvas.

"Low tide in the salt marsh," she said, at last.

Liam hated low tide.
Low tide was mud, rotten egg smells,
and no boogie boarding.

Mom usually painted lighthouses,
sunsets, and seagulls.
The tourists loved her art
of the Jersey Shore.

"Cool," he said, to cheer her up.
"I don't know . . ." Her voice trailed away.

"How about a lemon slushy?"
Liam made awesome lemon slushies.

Mom finally smiled.
"I'd love one."

CREEPY

Liam couldn't stop
      thinking about
the giant eels.

So huge . . . and creepy.

What if one slid
      inside
      the cottage?

What if an eel slipped
      into
      Liam's bed?

MOM

wrinkled her brow at the word "eel."

"I don't like eels.
        I don't like anything about them."

Mom liked butterflies and birds.

        She liked things that fly,
                make nests,
                        look colorful,
                or sing songs.

Or else, maybe eels reminded her
        of Gramps, and the time
                he brought one home.

HIDE IN THE SAND

Last summer,
      before he got too sick,
      Gramps caught an eel
            in Blackwater Creek.

"They hide in the sand during the day.
Don't know why this one took my bait."

He dropped the eel in his fishing pail
      so Liam and Mom
            could have a look.

FISH

Gramps said
the American eel
was a fish.

It didn't look
like any fish
Liam had ever seen.

It had a long body,
pointed head,
and small black eyes.

The eel looked more
like a snake.

Or maybe a fish-snake.
Or maybe a marsh monster!

SLIME

The eel arched
and flipped around
in the pail.

Liam reached out
to touch it.

"It grosses me out!"

The eel's greenish skin
was covered
in gooey slime.

"Mucus," Gramps said.

Liam had to scrub
hard to get the mucus
off his hand.

"Something's not right
with that eel," Gramps said.

He threw it
back in the creek.

The eel rippled
like a snake
through the water.

And then it was gone.

OUTER SPACE

Sunset in the salt marsh
happened in slow motion.

First the sun dropped
in the west.

White clouds turned to purple.
The steamy air cooled off.

A brown pelican dove for a fish.
A turtle swam to shore.

The last sounds were chirping crickets.

And then the fireflies
came out—

blinking stars
dancing over the night marsh.

Outer space on Earth.

GLOWING STAR

Was Gramps up there, somewhere—

like a blinking firefly
or a glowing star—

watching what was going on

down below?

Maybe Gramps wouldn't mind
Liam reading his journal.

Maybe he would actually
want Liam to read it.

TRY HARDER!

The door stuck like someone used superglue.

"Try harder!" Ciela hissed.

Liam twisted the knob again.

The damp air had bent the door.

"Let's forget about it," Liam said.

"Move away."

Ciela pushed her shoulder against the door.

All at once, Liam was staring

into his grandfather's bedroom.

HIDING PLACE

The air smelled stale.

Layers of dust
        had settled over everything —
the starfish quilt on the bed,
        the compass on the dresser,
the fishing boots by the closet,
        the binoculars on the window.

"Here it is!"
        Ciela had opened
        the top drawer of the dresser.

She held up a small black notebook.

        "How did you know where it was?"

"Same place I hide mine."

GRAMPS'S JOURNAL, JULY 1

Caught an eel in Blackwater Creek.

Don't know why the eel was active.
Thought eels slept by day.

Looked strange, too.

Liam wanted to touch it.

Oh boy, was he surprised!

Note to Self:

The eels in the creek could be in trouble.
Must find out why.

TROUBLE

"She's home!"

Mom's car tires crunched
on the seashell driveway.

Liam shoved the journal in the dresser
and they ran outside to the deck.

Gramps thought the eels
were in trouble—

But what kind of trouble?

"Your gramps was a cool writer," Ciela said.

TOMATOES

Mom invited Rosie for supper—gazpacho soup!
Rosie brought fresh tomatoes from her garden.

Liam wanted to talk about Gramps,
but Mom was having none of it.

Instead, they talked about Mom's new painting.
Low Tide in the Salt Marsh.

The canvas was mostly brown mud.
Kind of like Mom's mood all summer.

Rosie tapped her cane.
"Not sure the tourists will like that one."

Coco pecked Liam's ear.
"Handsome boy!" she squawked.

"Another great beach day
down the shore.
It's 93 degrees and sunny.
No rain in the forecast.

But listen to this:

People are reporting
strange wildlife
in Sandy Cove.

Some say they're eels.
Some say they're marsh monsters!

Sandy Cove Mayor Franco
says it's all a bunch of rumors.

'No one has proved
anything,' she told us.

'Sandy Cove is safe
and open for business!'"

SOMETHING WAS WRONG

While Mom went jogging
on Beach Road,

Liam grabbed
the journal again.

He noticed the dates
were the last month
of Gramps's life.

JULY 13

The more I think
about it,

something
was wrong
with that eel.

Its head
was too large.
Its body
was swollen.

Note to Self:
What could cause these problems?

HIGH SWELLS

The first good surf in July.
> High swells and white caps.
Sandy Cove Beach rocked with boogie boards.

Liam caught a perfect swell—
> smooth and fast—
the best wave all summer.

Just then, shouts exploded
> behind the lifeguard stand.
"Catch it!" a lady screamed.

Liam landed just in time.
> He saw a greenish tail
slither into the ocean.

"What the heck was that?"
> Matt the lifeguard ran off with the crowd.
"This beach is officially closed!"

THE LOOKOUT

Four days of rain.
No boogie boarding.
Liam was stuck inside.

Gramps had built
the wooden cottage
with his own hands.

Instead of an attic,
he wanted a lookout
on the third floor.

The small square
room had windows
on all sides.

Liam's favorite
place to sit and think
on rainy days.

Rain spattered the windows.
Liam turned on his laptop
and googled "eel."

SARGASSO SEA

This is what he read:

"The American eel
starts its life in the Sargasso Sea.

The sea lies off the East Coast
in the North Atlantic.

The cold, calm sea
is surrounded by warm,
fast currents.

Golden seaweed
covers the sea like blankets.

American eels swim
hundreds of miles
to feed on the seaweed.

They lay their eggs,
and then they die.

Millions of eggs hatch—

And then the tiny young eels
float many miles to shore."

LIAM LEARNED . . .

Adult eels are predators
that hunt at night.

They chase fish,
frogs, clams, insects,
and crabs.

With their sharp teeth,
they attack fast.

When day comes,
eels hide in sand and mud,
and under rocks.

*So why were the eels in
Sandy Cove crawling
around during the day?*

*Those sharp teeth
sound nasty!*

COMING OVER

Liam's cell phone buzzed.
"Can I come over?" Ciela asked.

"This time you ask first?"

Googling made his head hurt.

"Umm, not really.
I'm at the dock."

JAPANESE FAN

"Why do you even care
about the eels?"

Ciela had told him
she and her dad never live
in one place for very long.

Now, Ciela stood on the dock.

> She threw
> a pebble
> in the creek.

A circle of waves spread out
like a Japanese fan.

"Because," she said.
"Maybe, this time, we'll stay."

She threw another pebble.

"But only if it's safe around here.
My dad's worried."

SAFETY

Liam shivered under the hot sun.

If Sandy Cove wasn't safe

for blue crabs and eels,

was it safe for anyone?

MY HEART

Not feeling so good today.
The doc says it's my heart.
Rosie says it's the marsh.

Like my heart, it's getting weaker.
How much longer will the marsh—
and my heart—survive?

Liam closed the journal.

That was enough for today.

PART 2

NOT A LIE

"Did someone go in Gramps's room?"

Mom called upstairs to the lookout.

"Liam?"

He held his breath.

"Did you hear me?"

Pretending

not to hear

Mom's question

wasn't exactly

lying.

"I want that door to stay shut."

TREASURE CHEST

The crab pot banged
against Gramps's dock.
An empty treasure chest.

MAYBE

Ciela: My dad said that eels eat blue crabs.

Liam: Or maybe the blue crabs are dying and the eels are turning into monsters because the world's all messed up.

Ciela: Hmm.

Liam: By the way, are you ever going to ride a boogie board?

Ciela: I have to learn to swim first.

Liam: So why don't you?

Ciela: Maybe I am learning.

Liam: I'll believe it when I see it.

Ciela: By the way, my dad wants to meet you.

Liam: Nice subject change. But okay.

SHADY ACRES TRAILER PARK

"Turn here!" Ciela shouted.

The sign said, "Shady Acres Trailer Park."

Liam's bike skidded on stones.

No wonder the trailer park was called "shady."

Sky-high sugar maples,

masses of blackberry bushes,

out-of-control black-eyed Susans.

Almost every trailer had a vegetable garden.

Six-foot-tall sunflowers

stood guard in front of

a small, green trailer

shaped like a lime.

"Welcome to my castle," Ciela said.

TRAILER

The trailer felt
a lot bigger inside.

> Neat kitchen.
> Small metal table.
> Comfortable couch.

Over the couch
hung a photograph
of a man holding
a large, pink shell.

> "That's my dad,"
> said Ciela.

Then she pointed to the door.
"And so is that."

> A man in a black wet suit
> held a net with a fish.

"I almost got it," he said.

SOMETHING WRONG

Ciela's father, Luis,
had been diving for eels
all morning.

> Finally, he spotted
> a big one crawling
> on a rock.

Before he could
swing his net,
the eel slid away.

> Luis shook his head
> "Something was wrong
> with that eel."

ABUELO

Luis fried the fish for lunch.

While they ate,
              he told them
          about diving
                    for a shipwreck
              off South Carolina
          and chasing
                    great white sharks
              off Cape Cod.

Then he looked at Liam.

          "Sorry about your abuelo.
              We need him now."

Who told Luis about Gramps?

"The lady with the parrot."

Rosie, again.

ACCIDENT

On Friday, a truck almost
smashed an eel
next to the tourists on the boardwalk.

The truck hit a pole.
The eel slipped down a drain.
And the tourists freaked out!

Luckily, no one was hurt.
Mayor Franco called for a village meeting.
A secret village meeting.

"No reporters,
no cameras,
no cell phone videos," the mayor said.

Rosie rolled her eyes
"Don't let the tourists find out!"

Things were getting serious.

STANDING ROOM ONLY

Voices shook the meeting room at Village Hall.

The postman had been bitten. Twice.
Goldfish in the pond were missing.
A teenager found an eel in her fish tank.

Mayor Franco rapped her gavel.

"We've had a lot of reports about the eels.
Nobody's caught one yet,
as far as I know.

Am I right?"

From the back, a voice piped up.
"I've got one right here!"

Mom sighed. "For heaven's sake!"

BERNIE THE BAIT GUY

sold worms, crickets, and minnows
    at the Bait Shack on Beach Road.
Gramps was a regular customer.

Bernie stood up, lifting a glass tank.
    "He's eating me out of house and home."
Everyone turned to look.

"That's no eel," shouted the postman.
    "That's a water snake!"
The crowd erupted like a Yellowstone geyser.

"Fake news! We need facts!"
    Liam knew that voice.
Gramps's old friend, Mr. Burr.

1-800-555-EELS

Mayor Franco announced
a village hotline
for reporting eels.

She asked people
to take videos
and photographs.

"We need proof!

And everybody, please,
keep this quiet.

We don't want
to scare the tourists!"

68

GRAMPS'S JOURNAL
JULY 15

Took the skiff out
this morning with Liam.
Didn't catch anything,
except mosquito bites.

The water must be
80 degrees.
Too warm for July.
Could be driving the fish away.
Making other wildlife
act crazy.

Note to Self:

Who ever thought a power plant
in a salt marsh was a good idea?!

ENORMOUS!

"Look out!" Liam croaked like a marsh frog.

A giant eel was gliding

next to the kayak

in Blackwater Creek.

It was enormous!

Six feet long, at least.

Muscles bulged under its skin.

If that eel flipped its tail, they were sunk!

DUD

"Take a picture, fast!" Ciela shouted.

Mayor Franco said they needed photos.

Mr. Burr said they needed facts.

A photo could provide important facts.

Liam grabbed his cell phone. Click!

A blur.

A ripple.

The eel was gone.

A 21st-century cell phone camera

was no match

for an American eel.

FISHING SKIFF

When they got to the dock,
Liam saw Mom in the garage.

She was staring at
Gramps's old fishing skiff.

Liam was so shocked,
his paddle splashed Ciela's face.

"Can you guys help me?" Mom called.
"The skiff belongs in the water."

So, Mom hadn't
forgotten about Gramps!

They helped roll
the skiff down to the creek.

"Maybe you can take
it out someday, Liam."

Liam could never ride
the skiff without Gramps.

FISHING WITH GRAMPS

Gramps was an architect,
      not a fisherman.
But fishing was what he loved.

After he retired, he went
      fishing out in the marsh
almost every day.

He only caught fish
      for the family to eat.
Always threw back the small ones.

In his skiff, Gramps didn't look
      angry or frustrated.

He didn't rant or rave.

He looked peaceful—
      and he made Liam
feel peaceful, too.

LUIS

On Saturday, Luis knocked
on the cottage door.

"I was in the creek
last night at sunset.
Saw a giant eel catch a blue crab.
Chewed it up, shell and all.
Never seen that before.
Usually they only eat soft shells.
Ciela said you'd want to know.
Facts, and all that.
Don't worry.
Never heard of an eel
attacking a human.
Not yet anyway.
Could give you a heart
attack, though!
That eel didn't
look right."

Mom didn't look
right, either.

She looked
as greenish
as an eel.

GRAMPS'S JOURNAL
JULY 25

Not feeling too well. Stayed in bed all day.
Got Liam to teach me to use his laptop.

Love that Google thing.

The world at my fingertips!

Did you know?

Eels can live more than 40 years.
They live in fresh water and salt water.
They travel on land
by breathing through their skin.

Note to Self:

But can eels survive our foolishness?

FROM GLASS TO SILVER

Liam kept googling, too.

"After eggs hatch in the Sargasso Sea,
 the *larvae* floats on ocean currents
 to the coast.

The larvae turn into tiny ***glass eels***.

When the ***glass eels*** reach shore,
they swim upstream.
Their skin darkens
and they're called elvers.

Young American eels
live in marshes, ponds,
and rivers for many years.

At last, the long,
muscular ***silver eels***
swim back to the Sargasso
Sea to lay their eggs."

YOUNG EELS

If only people could change
like eels.

Maybe Mom could talk
about Gramps.

Maybe Ciela could learn
to swim.

Maybe Liam could
figure out how to let Gramps go.

Then Liam had a terrible thought:

The giant eels around Sandy Cove
were not silver yet.

They were young eels.

They had time to grow even bigger.

POST OFFICE

Ever since the eel
got in their mailbox,
Mom picked up the mail
at the post office.

On Wednesday, she ran
into Mr. Burr mailing a letter.

"Mr. Burr said something
about chicken livers,"
Mom told Liam
when she got home.

"What does that mean?"

Also, Aunt Cissy had sent
a postcard from Rome.

Luckily, no one had
chewed up the Colosseum.

BIG SWELLS

"Liam, is that you?"
Rosie's voice boomed on Gramps's landline.
"Big swells this morning!'

"Really?"
Liam knocked over his orange juice
when he jumped up from the kitchen table.

Then he remembered—
   Mom wanted him to paint the side fence.
   An all-day job.

No big swells for Liam.

SWEAT

The red kayak banged into the dock.
Ciela, again?
She was so annoying!

"You look funny!" she yelled.
Sure, funny.

Liam was sweating buckets
and his brown hair was speckled
with white paint.

"Need any help?"

Liam didn't want to see Ciela.
      He also didn't want
        to talk about giant eels.
All he wanted
      was to catch
      some good waves
      before the tide went out.

"Hey," he called back.
"You know zombies
aren't real, right?"

Ciela's hand flew up
to her bandage.

"And I don't need your help!" he said.

LOSER

Done, at last.

Liam grabbed his board
and jumped on his bike.

Beach Road was one

      long,

      hot,

      honking,

      traffic

      jam.

By the time Liam got to the beach,
    the wind had died
    and the swells were gone.

"Slowpokes are losers!"
shouted Matt the lifeguard.

LET DOWN

Liam wasn't mad at Ciela.

He was mad at himself
        for not trying harder
to figure out what was happening
        in the salt marsh.

He was letting Gramps down.

AT RISK

That night, Liam googled
"eel" again.

He found an article
in *Green Earth* News.

"Eels are a strong species.
They have survived
for millions of years.

But climate change is real.

The future of eels
and all marine animals
is at risk."

CHICKEN LIVERS

"What do you want?"

Ciela stood in the doorway
of the lime-green trailer.

She was not smiling.

Guess she hadn't forgotten
the other day.

"We need chicken livers,"
Liam said.

"Eww! Chicken livers!"

She hopped on her bike.

FAKE

Liam stared at Ciela.

Her bandage was off.

Her ear was red and swollen.

"Why did you say a zombie bit you?" Liam asked.

"Because it did," she said.

"Zombies are fake. They're stupid."

"Yeah, and so are you."

To tell the truth,
her ear did look like a zombie bit it.

"Why do we need chicken livers?"

"Mr. Burr said they're bait for eels."

BAIT SHACK

Tanks of minnows and boxes of crickets
filled the roadside shack.

Bernie was counting worms in a crate.
"I miss your grandfather," he said.

"Yeah," said Liam. "Me, too."

"Do you sell chicken livers?" asked Ciela.

"Zombies like them," Liam joked.

Ciela turned red. "They're for the eels."

Bernie opened his mouth. He shut it.
He said to Ciela, "Did a zombie bite your ear?"

Liam couldn't believe his ears.

Bernie sold them a box of stinky chicken livers.
"Hope you catch one!"

Did he mean an eel, or a zombie?

FISHING FOR EELS

Hooking a chicken liver

onto a fishing line wasn't easy.

Three had slid through Ciela's fingers

and landed on the dock.

Plop! Another one fell on her shorts.

"Disgusting!" she shouted.

"Slimy and slippery like eels," said Liam.

"Maybe that's why eels love 'em."

NO BITES

It was no use.

Two hours of fishing from the dock—
and not a single bite.

"I don't think eels
want to get caught," Liam said.

"Or else, they've
gotten so weird,
they don't
like chicken
livers
anymore," said Ciela.

Goosebumps rose on Liam's arms.

PART 3

RED LIST

Liam's Google searches
kept turning up new facts:

"In 2014, the International Union
for the Conservation of Nature
put the American eel
on the red list of endangered species."

When Liam told Ciela,
she shook her head.

"Everybody here
is scared of the eels.

They want to get rid
of them.

Maybe we really
need to protect them.

If something's gone
wrong with them,
it's probably our fault."

Gramps would say
that Ciela
was probably right.

THE LAST HURRICANE

Lying in bed, Liam remembered something.

> Something about the last big hurricane.
> Two weeks before Gramps passed.

Beach dunes washed away.
Rosie's Art Tent blew over.
A tree fell on Gramps's deck and fence.

> The Blackwater Creek Power Plant
> flooded badly.

With no electricity,
everybody's lights were out for days.

BALONEY

Liam snuck into Gramps's room,
       and grabbed the journal again.

He turned to the page dated July 30.

The day the hurricane
       moved out into the Atlantic Ocean.

Gramps had pasted a clip from the *Shore News*:

"The hurricane floods
caused a small amount of fuel
to leak from the power plant.

There is no need for public concern.

"A small leak. Fixed quickly," the plant manager
said.
"No real problem," Mayor Franco said.
"No cause for panic," the governor said.

In Gramps's own handwriting were three words:

Baloney. Baloney. Baloney.

CROOKS

Gramps was getting weak by then.

He stayed in bed most of the day.
Mom moved the TV into his room,
so he could watch the news.

Gramps had forgotten some of his words.
But not all of them.

He had not forgotten "baloney"
and other favorite phrases.

And, when the news lady
talked about the power plant,

Liam heard Gramps say, clear as day,

"Those dirty crooks!"

TORNADO

Missing crabs.

Giant eels.

Climate change.

Hurricanes.

Leaks from a nuclear power plant.

Crooks and baloney.

Liam's brain felt like a tornado had hit it.

What he needed was advice.

From somebody who knew about science.

Somebody who knew that facts mattered.

HORSESHOE CRABS

Last spring, Liam's science teacher,
Mr. Tyger, took the class on a field trip
to see the horseshoe crabs.

Liam would never forget what he saw.

Hundreds of horseshoe crabs
climbing out of the ocean.

Burying themselves in the sand.
And then laying their eggs.

"And, get this," Mr. Tyger had told the class.
"Horseshoe crabs have been laying eggs
on this very same beach
since long before the dinosaurs
roamed New Jersey."

How awesome!

EMAIL

If Mr. Tyger knew about horseshoe crabs,
he might know about eels.

"I'm going to write my science teacher a letter,"
Liam told Ciela.

They were in the lookout.
Ciela loved it there.
She said it was like being part of the sky.

"Email is a lot faster."

DEAR MR. TYGER,

We need your advice.
Could a leak at the Blackwater
Creek Power Plant
change the wildlife in the salt marsh?
We're talking about blue crabs and eels.

Your student,
Liam Baker

About 10 minutes later, Mr. Tyger wrote back.

DEAR LIAM,

I am glad you asked that question.
You're right.
A leak from the plant could harm wildlife.
But you need more facts.
What have you seen so far?

Your teacher,
Mr. Tyger.

"Can I answer him?" Ciela asked.

Dear Mr. Tyger,

The eels are giant.
They look weird, too.
They are at the beach and in the market.
My dad is worried they might give someone
a heart attack.
What should we do?

Liam's friend,
Ciela

P.S. As for the blue crabs, there aren't any!

Two minutes later, the email mailbox clicked.

DEAR LIAM AND CIELA,

How are they keeping this out of the news?
I hope the power plant has been careful.
Leaks and overflows are dangerous!
Climate change is also affecting wildlife.
Be careful. You must investigate.
I am leaving on my vacation, so I can't be of much help.
I believe in you two.

Your teacher,
Mr. Tyger

DRAGONFLY

"Your teacher is right," Ciela said later.

They were cleaning out the kayak by the dock.

"I just don't know what we should do," Liam answered.

Just then, a dragonfly swooped like an acrobat past Ciela's shoulder.

It reminded Liam of boogie boarding.

Boogie boarding always helped him to think more clearly.

"Let's go to the beach," Liam said.

"Only if we can get Italian ice," Ciela said.

Liam never said no to Italian ice.

BREAKING WAVE

The wave lifted him up
and threw him down.

He tumbled in the salt water
like a sneaker in a washing machine.

This was NOT helping him
think more clearly!

Good thing Ciela was
up the boardwalk with Rosie.

A few minutes later,
Liam was drying off on the beach.

Ciela came running.

"Rosie says Mr. Burr has something
important to tell us!"

She handed him
a cherry-red Italian ice.

His favorite flavor.

"I wonder what."

COME SEE ME

The next morning, Gramp's landline
was ringing again.

Liam ran downstairs from the lookout.

"Come see me.
You and Ciela."

Mr. Burr hung up.

Rosie was right, again.

PROTEST!

Mr. Burr rocked on the porch
with his orange cat.

"I just remembered something," he told them.

"Back in the 1970s,
the power plant got your gramps
all fired up.

He was sure the plant
was dumping wastewater
in the marsh.

He called for a protest.

'We need to make a ruckus,'
your gramps said."

Mr. Burr nodded slowly.

"I can still hear his voice."

Liam could, too.

CLIMBING THE FENCE

"We made a ruckus, for sure," Mr. Burr went on.
"Rosie, Gramps, and I climbed the fence.
We dumped pails of red paint on the walls.

'Red for blood,' your grandfather said.
'The salt marsh's blood.'

Of course, the plant manager called the police."

"You were arrested?!" Ciela squealed.

FACTS, AGAIN

Mr. Burr stopped talking.
Had he fallen asleep?

But he was smiling
behind his white beard.

"We felt like the Boston Tea Party!"

He and Rosie and Gramps
were only in jail for a few hours.

Nothing changed after that, either.

"We couldn't prove anything.
No one ever could."

Facts, again.

"Everything Is Connected"

Gramps wrote in his journal on August 2.

Liam felt like
        the opposite was true.
Everything was broken.

The eels
        were crawling
out of the creek.

The blue crabs
        were missing.
Mom hardly ever smiled.

Even Ciela was acting strange.
She couldn't go kayaking tomorrow.

And she wouldn't tell Liam why.

MAP

Liam dropped off
one of Mom's sunset paintings
from last year
at Rosie's Art Tent.

"Young Liam, you're just
 the person I wanted to see!"

Coco was eating watermelon,
the exact same color
as Rosie's balloon dress.

Rosie handed Liam
a rolled-up paper.

"Your gramps gave me his map
the last time we went fishing.
I think you'll find it useful."

Rosie winked at him—
and Coco squawked, "Pretty bird!"

DANGERS

The next day, Liam woke up super early.
He needed *more* facts
in order to get *new* facts.

Opening his laptop,
he googled "Dangers to eels."

"Biggest dangers to eels:
Pollution
Disease
River dams
Power plants
Fishing"

Then he read this: "When waters warm up,
young eels and other fish may grow faster.
Their behavior may change, as well."

The biggest clue yet!

RED X

Blackwater Creek was like a maze.

With so many twists and turns,
it was easy to get lost!

Good thing they had Gramps's map.

Gramps had marked the power plant
with a red X.

The map showed the plant
at the northeast edge
of the salt marsh.

But one corner of
the map was missing.

The corner next
to the red X.

Gramps must have torn it off.

Why?

TURN HERE

They paddled for 30 minutes
until they could see the blue dome
of the power plant clearly.

It looked both near and far away.

"Turn here," Liam told Ciela.
He pointed to a small inlet on the left.

Liam's paddle swept forward.
Ciela's swept backward
on the opposite side.

The kayak turned neatly.

Their paddles sliced the water
at exactly the same time.

It was like they'd been
        kayaking together
                forever.

STUCK IN THE MUD

They followed the creek
way past Mom's one-hour deadline.

An osprey
dive-bombed them.

Mosquitoes
attacked them.

The marsh air
felt like an oven.

The kayak even got stuck in the mud.
Liam and Ciela had to jump out.

They dragged the kayak
back in the waterstream.

"We need to come back
at high tide," Liam finally said.

They didn't get anywhere
near the blue dome.

SORRY

Mom was waiting on the dock.

She was steaming mad.

"Where were you?"

Her arms were crossed.

"Sorry," Liam said.

"It won't happen again," added Ciela.

"No, it won't."

And Mom turned away.

"HELLO, FROM TOKYO!"

Aunt Cissy's latest postcard
showed a dish of food.

"The tastiest meal all summer!"
Aunt Cissy wrote. "It's called *unadon*."

Liam googled "unadon."

Grilled eel rice bowl.
A popular dish in Japan.

Aunt Cissy signed off.
"Miss you guys!"

Liam wasn't hungry
for the rest of the day.

CURFEW

One of Mom's friends
surprised an eel
in her toilet.

A giant eel
was spotted
at a youth soccer game.

It slid,
slithered,
and slipped away
into a stream.

Mayor Franco declared
a village emergency.
A curfew was set
for 7 p.m.

What had Gramps said to Liam?
*Something's wrong
with that eel.*

BLUE CRABS

Mom's copy of the *Shore News*
lay on the kitchen table.

"Vanishing Blue Crabs," said the headline.

A scientist from Rutgers University
said that "warming oceans
and higher temperatures
are a growing
threat to blue crabs
on the Jersey Shore."

Hungry eels aren't helping,
thought Liam.

What a mess!

TINY SNAILS

Mom's low tide painting was finished.
She propped it up on Gramps's green chair.

Liam was surprised.
The canvas wasn't just brown mud.

He could see . . .

Tiny snails.

A turtle's eggs.

The claw prints of a shorebird.

And in the bottom left corner—
a blue pipe.

BLUE PIPE

"Where is that pipe?" Liam asked Mom.

She shook her head.

> "I don't know.
> Gramps mentioned it
> a long time ago.
>
> He said the pipe
> could mean the end
> of the salt marsh."

Mom looked at her paint-covered hands.
> "You know, I miss your gramps a lot."

It was the first time
> Mom had said Gramps's name
> > in a very long time.

BLACK SKULL

After Mom was asleep,
Liam snuck into Gramps's room.

He opened the journal
to a page with no writing.

Just a scrap of colored paper.
The missing corner of the map.

Liam looked closely.

Gramps had drawn something.

A black skull.

THE SAME THING

It wasn't the power plant

Liam and Ciela had to get to.

It was the black skull

and the blue pipe.

Liam was pretty sure

the two were

the same thing.

PART 4

SANDBAGS

Mayor Franco had stopped talking about eels.
Now she was talking about wind, rain,
and flooding.

A tropical storm was aiming at the Jersey Shore.
She hoped it wouldn't be as bad as last year's
hurricane.

"Let's be prepared! Everyone needs to pitch in.
Remember, we're in this together."

Village trucks dropped sandbags
up and down Ocean Avenue.

Rosie packed up her Art Tent
and took Coco home.

Mom taped the windows
and bought extra gallons of water.

And Liam made sure Gramps's fishing
skiff was tied safely to the dock.

"Sandy Cove will ride the storm!"
Mayor Franco said.

Jersey Shore Radio: Storm Watch

"Tropical Storm Tufani
is traveling up the East Coast.

It has wind speeds of 40 miles per hour
and is moving at 13 miles per hour.

With warm ocean waters,
it could get stronger
over the next few days.

Stay tuned for more weather alerts—
and be prepared!

This storm is no joke, folks."

NOW OR NEVER

Up in the lookout,
Liam raised Gramps's binoculars.

The marsh grasses
waved in the breeze.
A seagull caught a fish
in the dark creek.

And the blue dome of the power plant
looked like a UFO
from another galaxy.

It had been over 50 years
since Gramps said the plant
was harming the marsh.
No one believed him.

It was time for Liam
to prove Gramps was right.

Storm, or no storm.

ONE HOUR

The sun was still shining
when Ciela picked up Liam
in her kayak.

He had Gramps's map
and compass in a
waterproof bag.

"We'll be back quickly,"
he promised Mom.

Mom crossed her arms.

"One hour, max.
I'll be waiting on the dock."

CHARCOAL CLOUDS

Just 20 minutes later, the sun was gone.

Clouds raced across the sky
like chunks of flying charcoal.

Angry gusts of wind churned the creek
like eggbeaters.

Ciela's hat sailed away.

"Let's turn around, Liam!"

Liam looked at the compass
and the map with the corner he'd glued on.

"Not yet!" he shouted back.

SAME DUCK

Gramps never got lost.

He knew the creek's ways
like his own body.

Too bad Liam
hadn't paid
more attention.

The compass
and the map
weren't enough.

Not with all
the twists and turns.

Not with the sun
disappearing.

Not with the storm
getting closer.

"Didn't we just see
the same duck
on the same rock?"

Ciela wasn't wrong.

FOUND

Ciela lifted her paddle
from the water.
"We're in trouble, aren't we?"

Liam didn't answer.

He was staring
at something poking
between the grasses
on the muddy shore.

You could easily miss it.
At high tide, it would be hidden.

But the tide was turning.
No more secrets.

The pipe looked exactly
like the one in Mom's painting.

FISH CHOWDER

Toward the end,
Mom's fish chowder
was the only food Gramps would eat.

One morning,
Gramps pushed
the spoon away.

"You gotta watch
out for them."

"Watch out
for who, Gramps?"

"The fools who think
they know what they're doing!"

HOT WATER

Water spurted out of the pipe
like a garden hose turned to jet spray.

Liam lay down his paddle.

He needed to know
if the water was cold or hot.

But he couldn't reach
his hand out far enough,

without slipping off
his life jacket.

That was his first mistake.

HOT ENOUGH

Liam leaned farther.

His fingers touched the spurting water.

Steaming hot!

Hot enough to burn his hand.
Hot enough to make eels weird.
Hot enough to kill blue crabs.
Hot enough to harm the whole salt marsh.

Then Ciela shouted.
"There are more of them!
I see two more pipes!"

SECOND MISTAKE

The kayak bobbed up
and down in the whitecaps.
Rain pounded harder.

Was the spurting water really that hot,
or had he imagined it?
Liam needed to be sure.

"What are you doing?
You're leaning too far!"

His second mistake.

His paddle slid into the creek.
Then he did, too.

The kayak had flipped over.

"Hold on!" Ciela screamed.
"Don't let go!"

LIKE AN EEL

Another gust, and the whitecaps
swallowed the kayak.

Leaving Ciela and Liam
struggling
to stay afloat.

To keep their heads above water.
To breathe.

(But not before Ciela snapped a picture
with her dad's waterproof, deep-sea camera.)

GRAB MY HAND

Liam: Are you okay?

Ciela: The kayak's gone!

Liam: I'm aware.

Ciela: I can't believe you
took off your life jacket.

Liam: I'm an idiot!

Ciela: Grab my hand!

Liam: I can swim.

Ciela: I said, grab my hand!

Liam: Okay. Please don't let go.

GRAMPS'S JOURNAL
AUGUST 12

The night before, Liam had read
Gramps's final page in his journal.

Note to Self:

> Take the temperature in the creek.
> Look for wastewater in the East Inlet.
> DANGER.

Three days later, he passed away.

NOT OKAY

Liam was trying to do what
　　　Gramps had wanted to do himself.

Find the answers.
　　　Make a difference.

Maybe everything *was* connected.
　　　That didn't make everything okay.

GRUMBLY VOICE

In the thick of the storm,
Liam heard Gramps's grumbly voice,

"Safety first.
Don't be a fool!"

If only Liam had listened harder.

FISHING SKIFF

Putt-putt-putt.
The sound was familiar.
Gramps's old fishing skiff.

Two figures in yellow raincoats
shouted over the howling storm.

"Liam! Ciela!"
Mr. Burr and Rosie.

The only person missing was Gramps.

Before the skiff could reach them,
Ciela screamed even louder.

"The zombie! It's going to eat you!"

And her hand slipped away.

GREENHEAD FLY

A greenhead fly

—not a zombie—

took a painful bite out of Liam's neck.

"OOWWWWWW!"

His head slipped
under the water.

ZOMBIES AREN'T REAL

The creek water churned with iron, salt —
                    and who knew what else?

Liam held his breath
                    until the greenhead fell off.

He held his breath
                    until he got dizzy and faint.

He held his breath
                    until his thoughts went wild . . .

            *Zombies aren't real,
            but other bad things are—*

            Gramps dying.

The power plant hurting the marsh.

                            Giant eels, everywhere.

And greenheads, of course.

EVERYTHING WENT BLACK

Reaching again for Ciela's hand,
     he felt nothing.

Gasping for air,
     he gulped water.

The tide was moving fast,
     dragging him to the ocean.

Another mouthful of water.

     Gag!
          Cough!

Everything went black.

NOT ALONE

"Liam!"

Three pairs of arms
lifted him out of the creek
and into the skiff.

With all the scary things
going on in the world,
Liam was glad he wasn't alone.

Jersey Shore Radio: Special Report

"Until it passes all safety tests,
Blackwater Creek Power Plant is shut down.

Overflows, leaks, and wastewater releases
are threatening the salt marshes.

The marsh is already fighting climate change.
Our precious treasure doesn't need more trouble.

Come on, Jersey Shore!
Let's get it together.
Save our marshes.
Save our wildlife.
Save our Earth."

DON'T LET THE FOOLS

Mom stood in the middle
of Gramps's bedroom.

"I can't believe everything
looks the same."

Liam pulled the journal
from the dresser drawer.

"Gramps helped us
figure everything out," he said.

Mom smiled. "It's almost like
he's still here with us."

He opened the journal.
A slip of paper fell out.

Together, they read aloud.
Don't let the fools win!

SUNSET FEAST

As the sun set over the salt marsh,

    an osprey flew along Blackwater Creek.

The last of the summer's greenheads

    searched for someone else to bite.

And a noisy feast

    got started on the back deck.

BLUEBERRY PIE

The picnic table was spread with:

Rosie's famous spicy chili,

Mr. Burr's fresh-picked sweet corn,

Mom's homemade blueberry pie,

Liam's ice-cold lemonade slushies,

and Ciela and Luis's sunflowers in a tall vase.

In between bites, everybody talked at once.

IF . . .

". . . Gramps hadn't mentioned the
blue pipe to Mom . . ."

"And if Liam hadn't seen the pipe
in the painting
        and found it in the marsh . . ."

"And if Ciela hadn't taken a picture of it . . ."

"And if Liam and Ciela hadn't marched into
Village Hall
and told Mayor Franco . . ."

"And if the governor hadn't ordered the
power plant
shut down until repairs and safety checks
were made . . ."

"I don't know where we'd all be now!"
Rosie finished.

"Gramps would be so proud of us!"

PRETTY CAT

Everyone was so busy
eating and talking.

No one noticed
Gramps's green chair
wasn't empty anymore.

Mr. Burr's cat made
little snoring noises.

"Pretty cat!" Coco squawked.

BREEZY DAY

at Sandy Cove Beach.

Seagulls swooped for picnic scraps.
        Whitecaps bubbled like ice cream sodas.
And Matt the lifeguard blew his whistle at Liam.

        "Got surf, buddy!"

Liam ran straight into the choppy ocean.

He threw himself onto his board,
                paddled with his arms,
        and kicked his feet.

Then he turned to wait for a wave.

LIME-GREEN BOOGIE BOARD

Someone was waving
        a lime-green boogie board
at him from the beach.

Ciela jumped in the water
        and kicked hard.

She really had been taking swim lessons!

Behind Liam, a wave was building.

        He paddled hard.
        Caught it!
        Smooth and clean.

Just as his feet touched sand,

        something slimy,
        slippery,
        and slithery
        slid over his right leg.

Ciela screamed.
"That is NOT seaweed!"

NOTE TO LIAM

After they cleaned out
Gramps's bedroom

and the charity truck
came to pick up

the bed and the dresser
to give to a family
who needed them,

Mom found one last
scrap of paper

floating in the dust balls—

Note to Liam:

The fishing skiff is yours.
Be safe out there!

Want to Keep Reading?

Here's a sneak peek at another book
from West 44 Books:

Daylan and the River of Secrets
by Edd Tello

ISBN#: 9781978597488

SOMEDAY

I dip my toes into
the green-blue water.
Then my whole body

                            sinks.

I'm no longer
Scaredy Daylan.
I flutter kick.
My arms move in circles
in the cold river.

                            I float.

The warm rays of the sun
shine on my face.

                            I dive.

"Daylan Torres, it's five.
Time to go!"

                          I open my eyes.

I am still sitting on the stones.

Mamá hugs me from behind.
Her long straight hair falls on my
sweaty forehead.

Someday, I tell myself.
Someday, I will dive into the river again.

NEWBORNS

I put my life jacket and
goggles in the trunk.
Mom towel-dries her hair.

By the way she stares at me,
I know she's worried.
I know both she and Papá
would like me to swim again.
It's been three years.

In San José Lagos,
water is sacred.
We swim from the time we are born.
Parents put their babies
in the clean waters of
the Nacimiento River.

> *Nacimiento* means "birth."
> People here also
> call the river *El Naci*.

I get into the car—
the same gray car
that Papá used to drive
before he left home.

CULEBRA

Dad left home
when I was nine.

For several months,
my parents' screams
were like a culebra
—a water snake.
They wound around my neck.

The fights happened more and more.
I felt as if a culebra
was dragging me
to the depths of El Naci.

One sunny afternoon,
Dad took me out
in this same car.

He said, sobbing,
"Sometimes relationships
don't work out.
You'll understand
when you grow up."

It's been three years,
and I still don't get it.

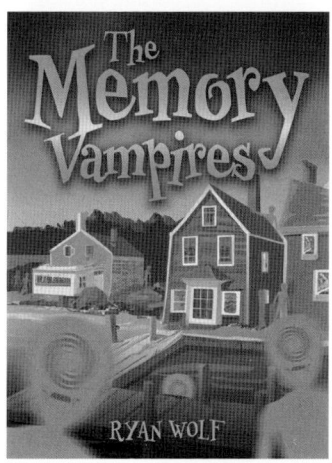

CHECK OUT MORE BOOKS AT:
www.west44books.com

ABOUT THE AUTHOR

Ann Malaspina often writes about the environment and social issues. LIAM AND THE GIANT EELS was inspired by visits to her brother's house on a saltwater marsh at the Jersey Shore, and the many young people fighting climate change around the globe.